" We wish this coloring book to be more than filled pages, but a magical portal that will transport you beyond the borders of space, where dreams come true and heaven is just the beginning."

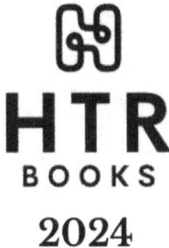

HTR
BOOKS

2024

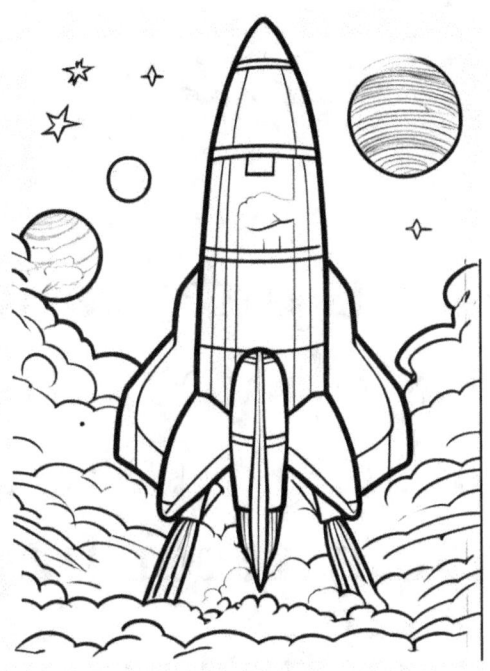

This Book Belongs to:

_____

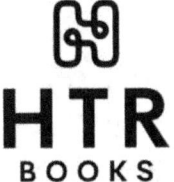

HTR
BOOKS

all rights reserved

ALL RIGHTS RESERVED©
2024

No part of this publication may be reproduced, distributed, or transmitted in any form or by any means, including photocopying, recording, or other electronic or mechanical methods, without the prior written permission of the publisher, except for brief quotations incorporated in critical reviews and other specific noncommercial uses. Any unauthorized replica of this work is prohibited.

Test Color Page

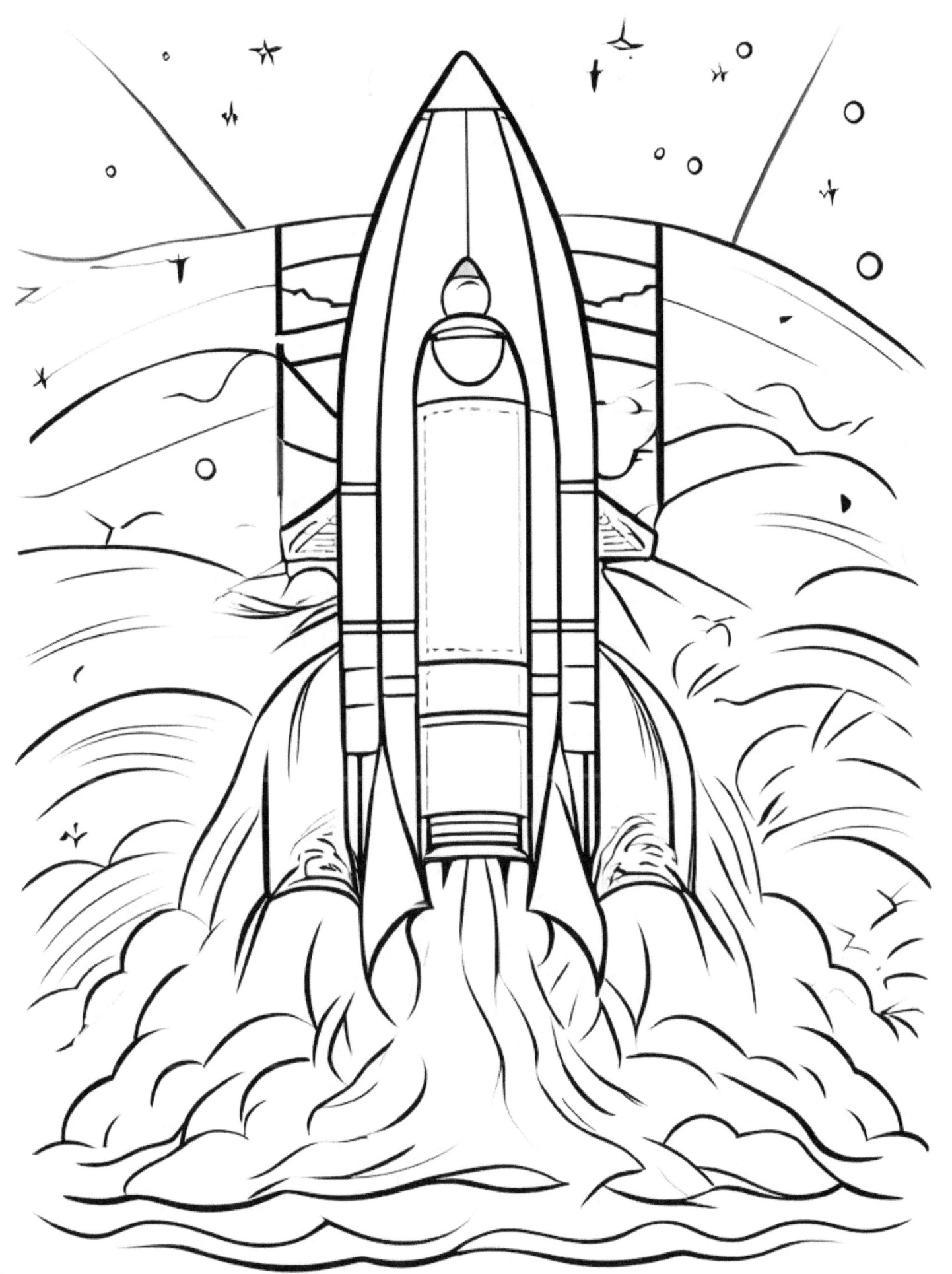

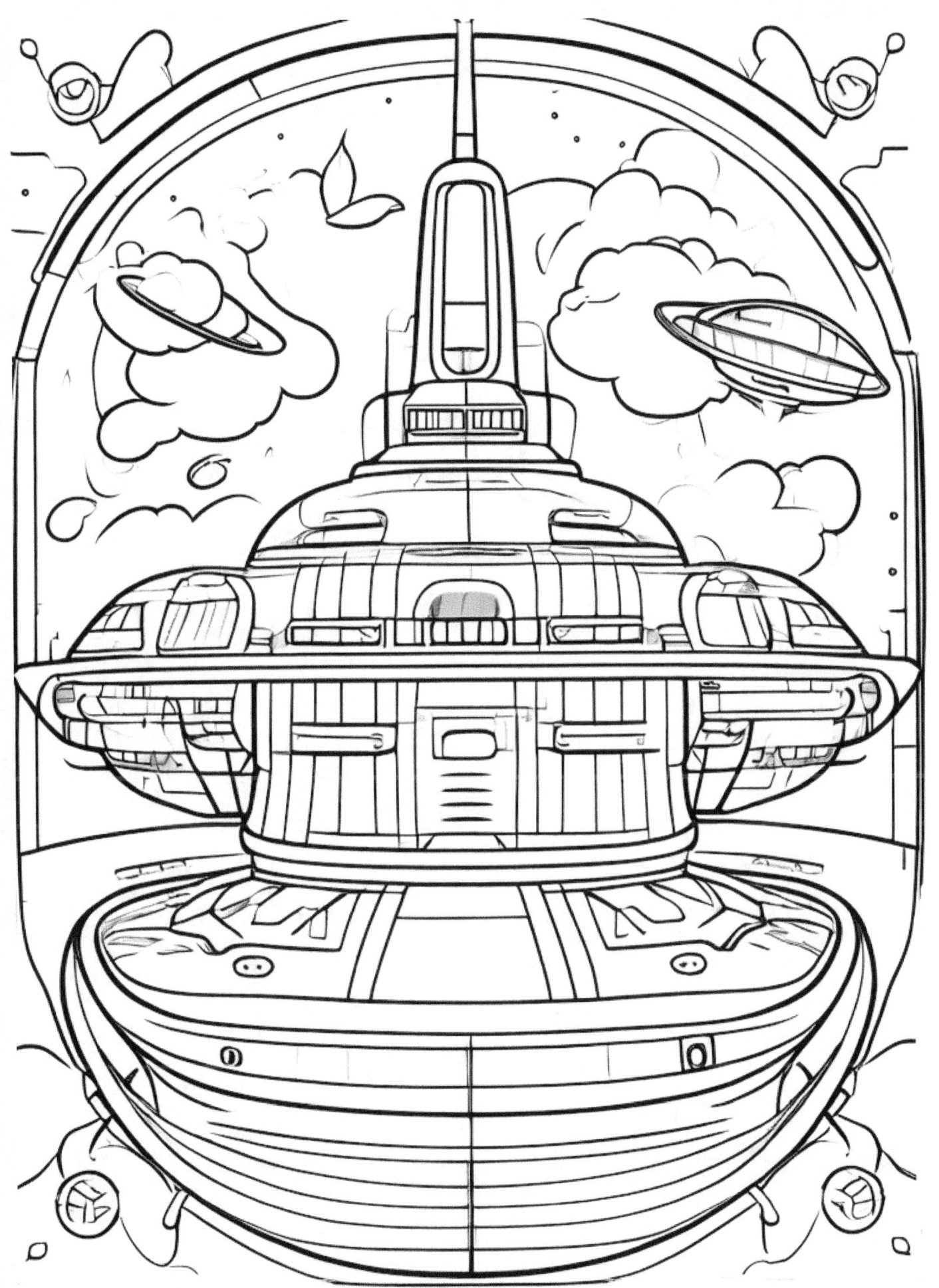

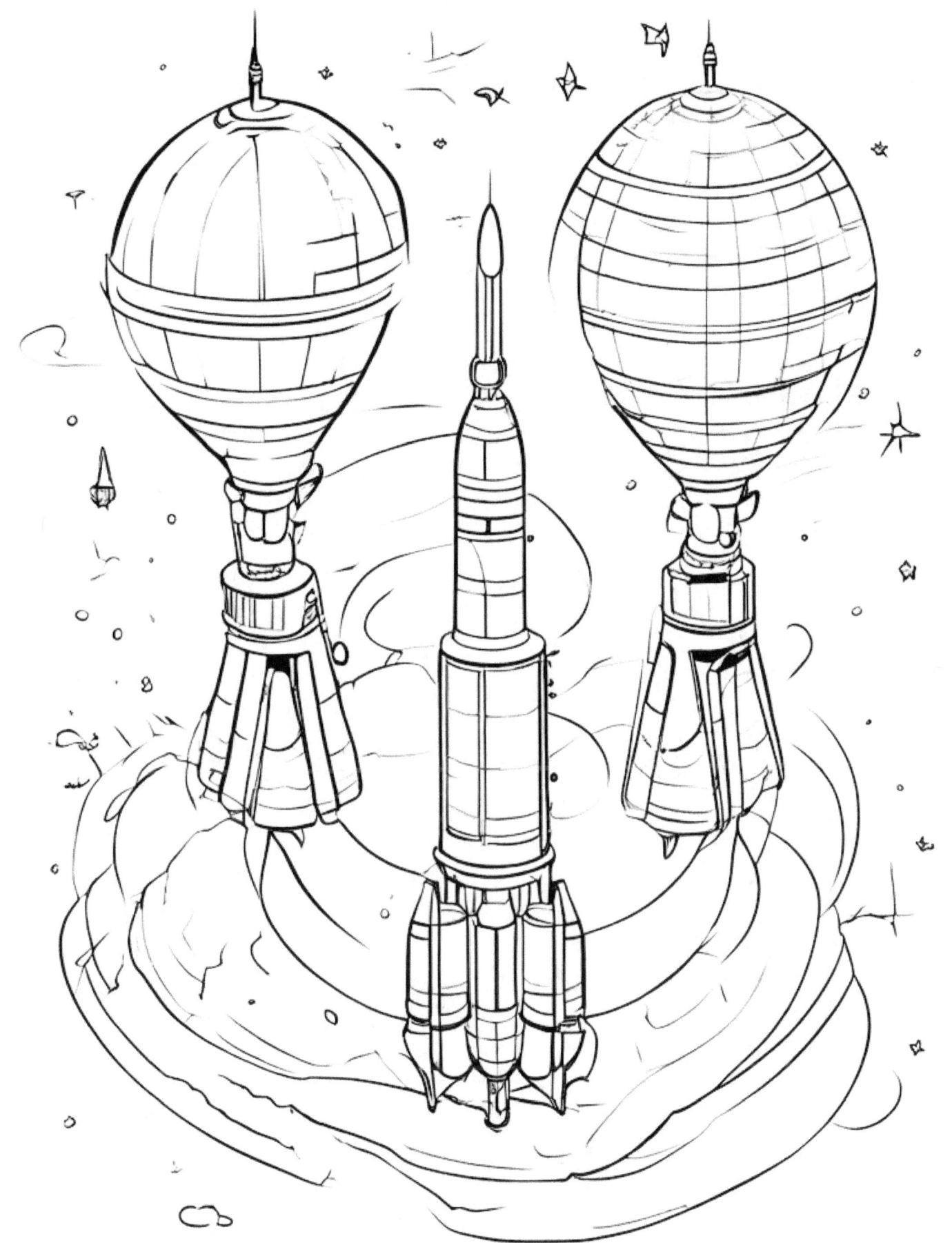

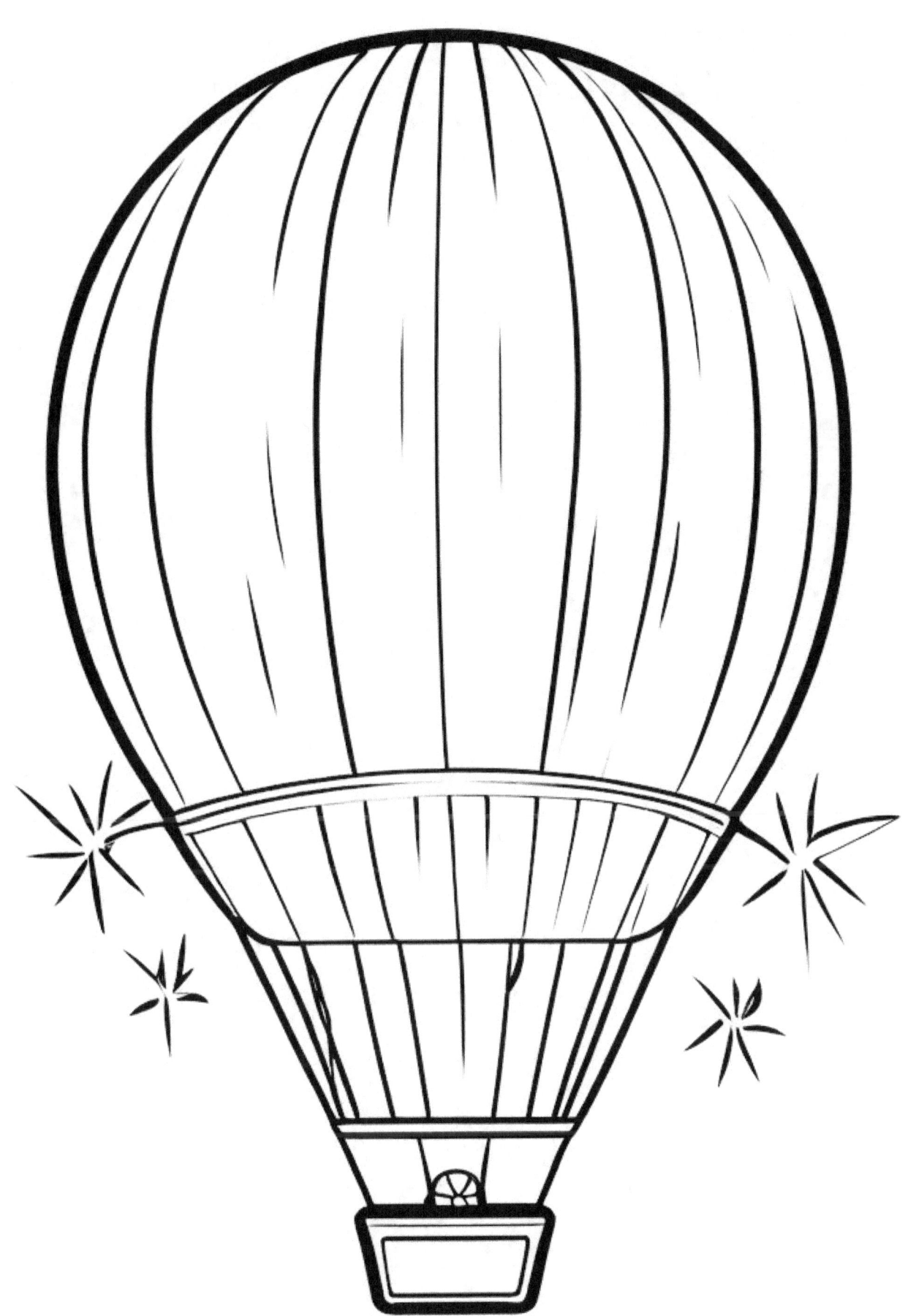

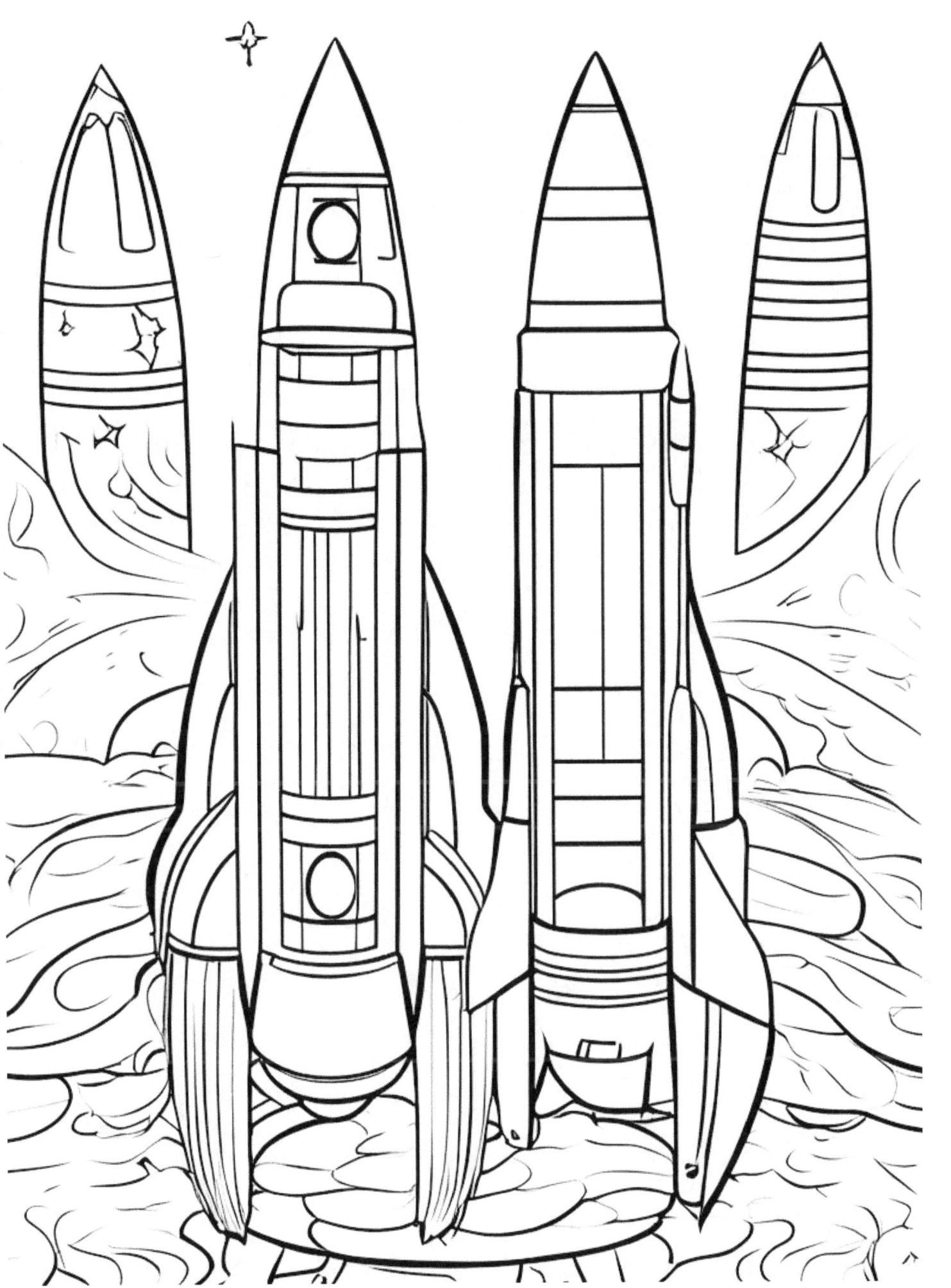

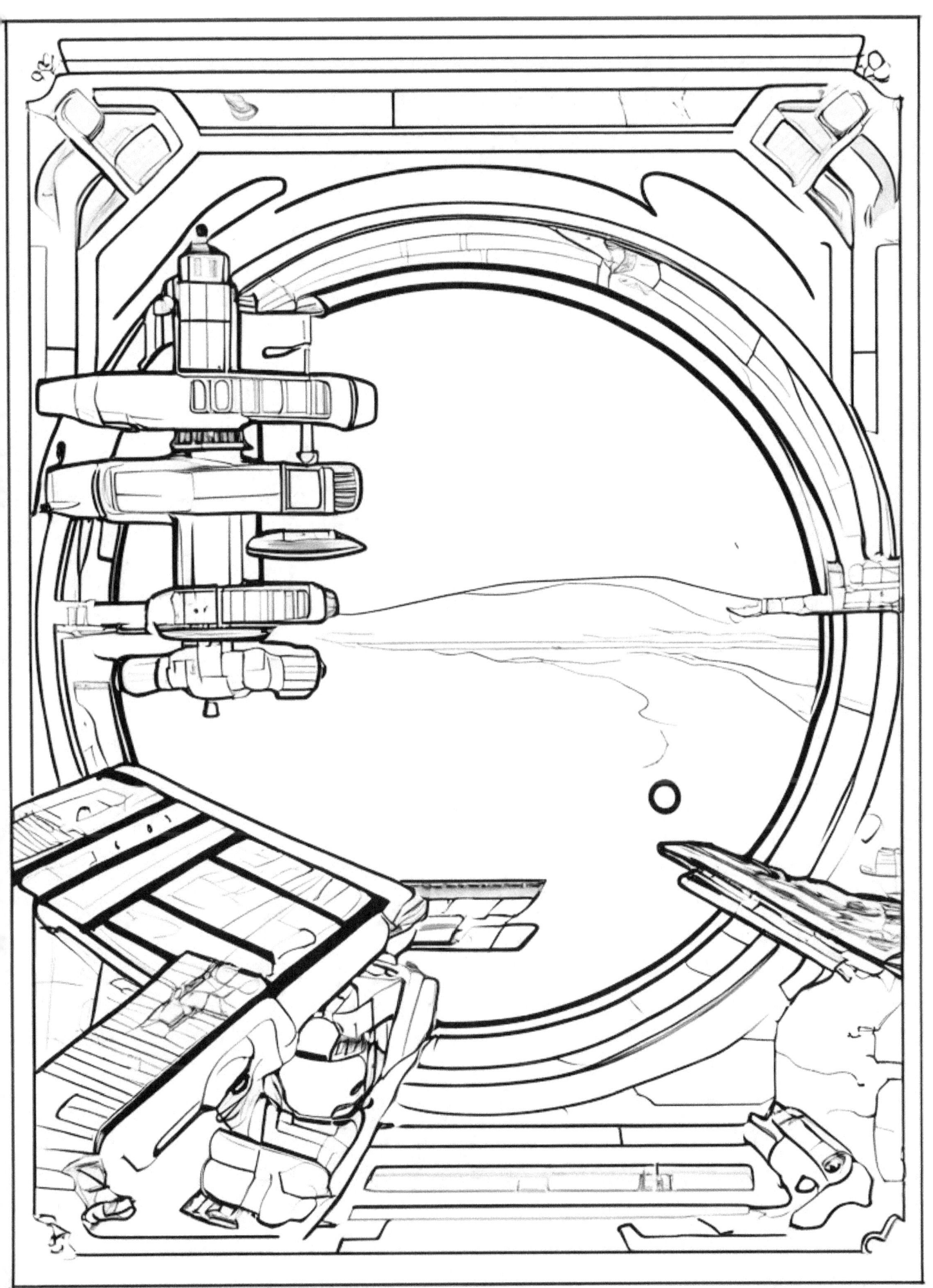

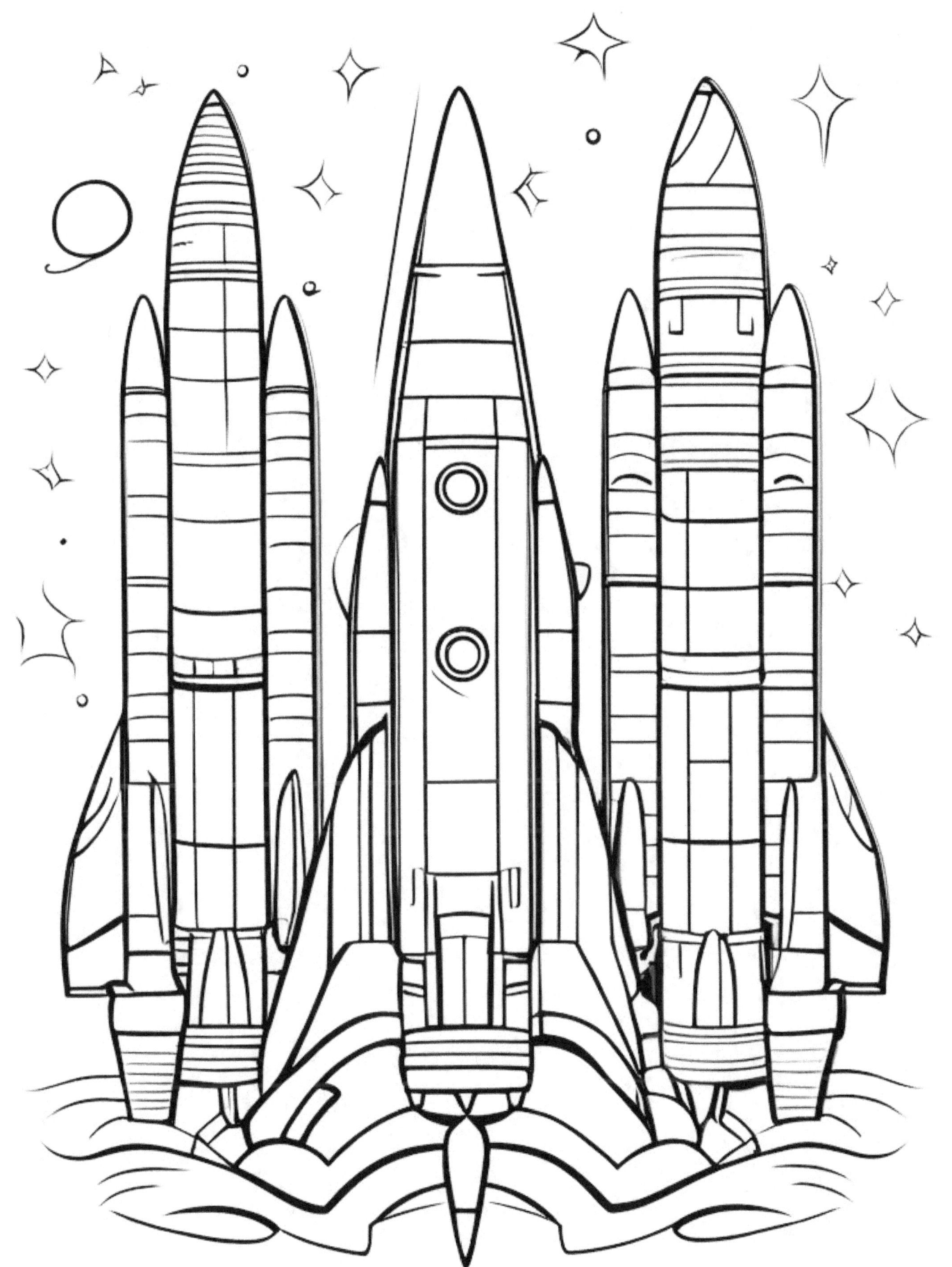

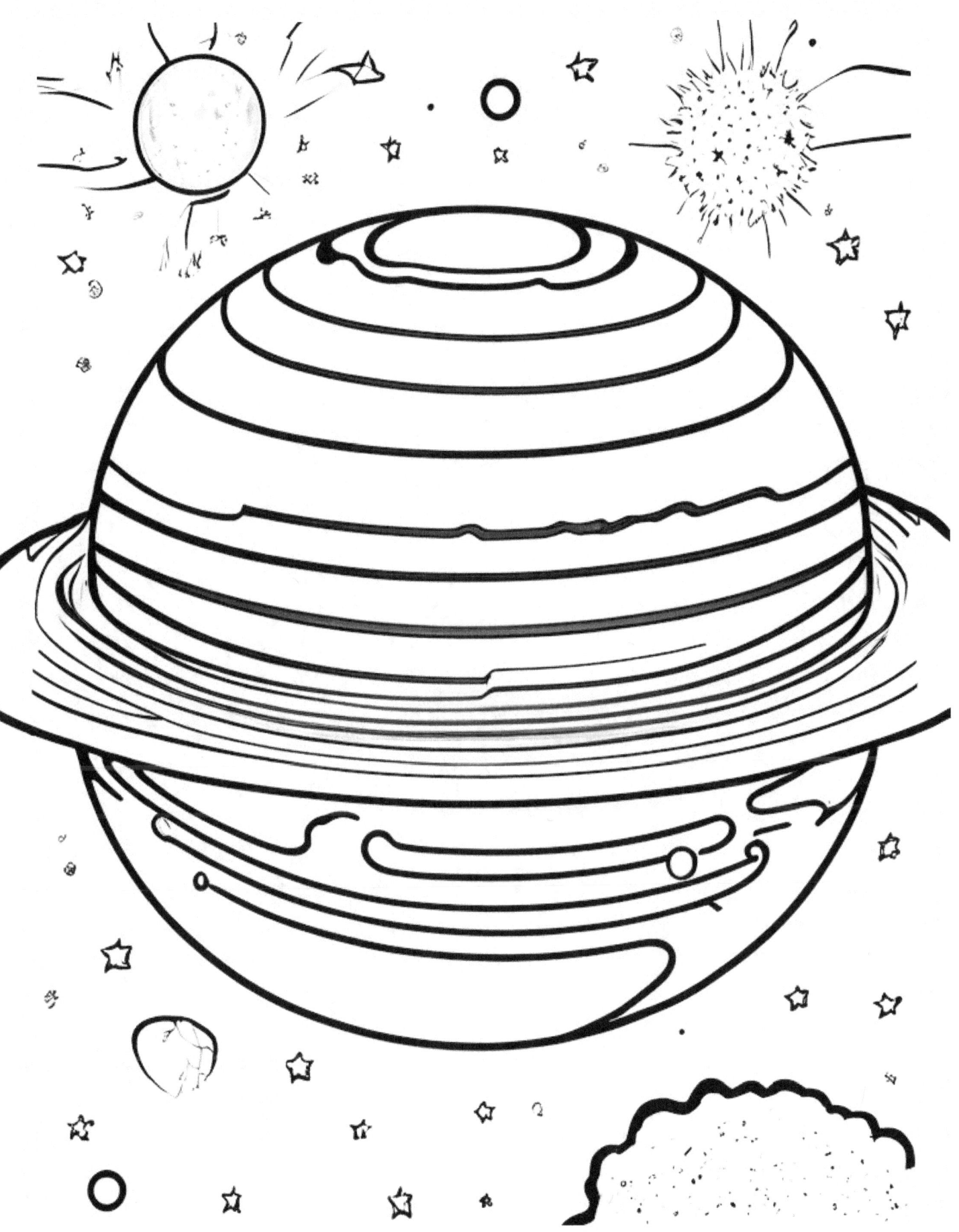

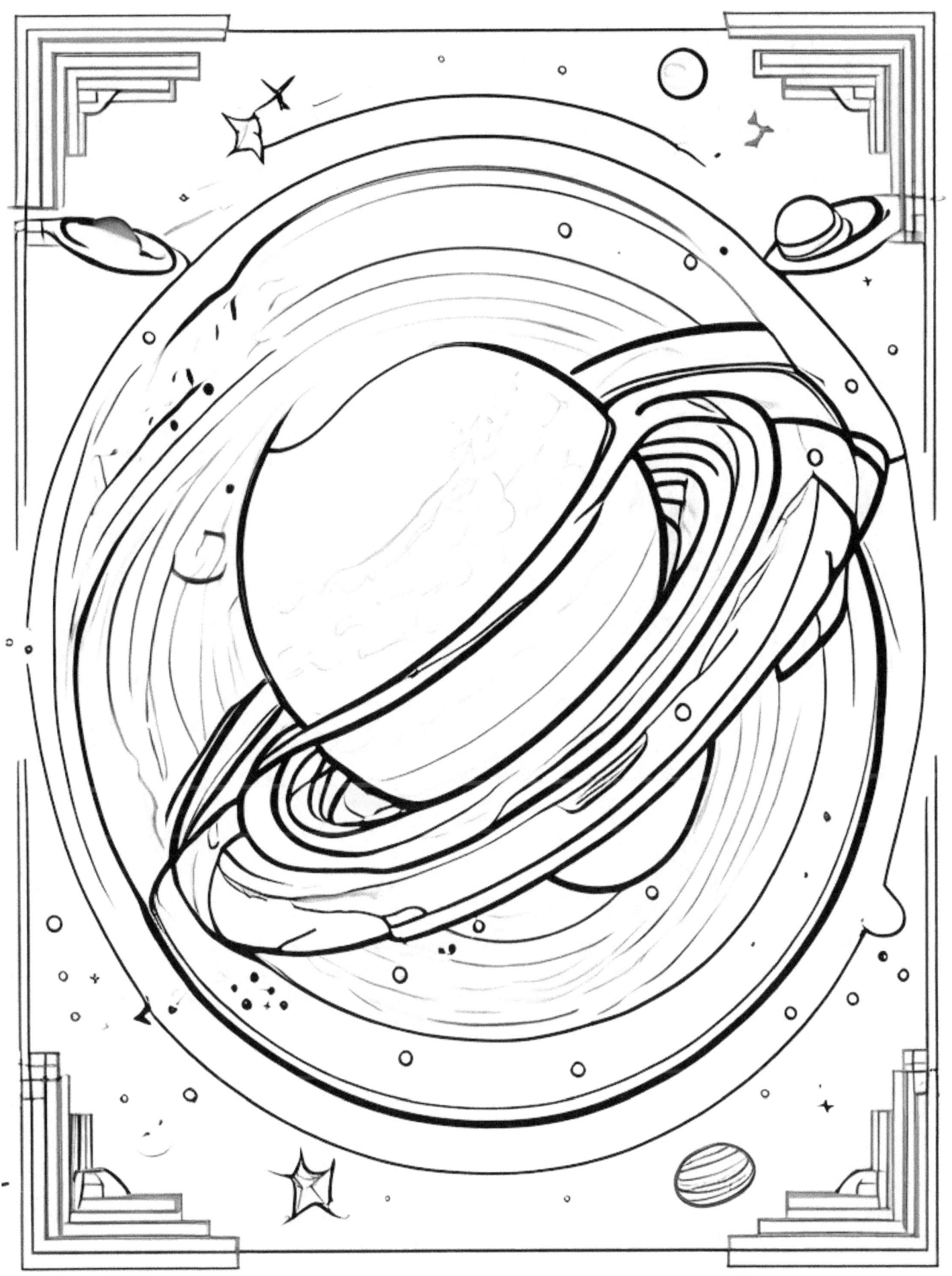

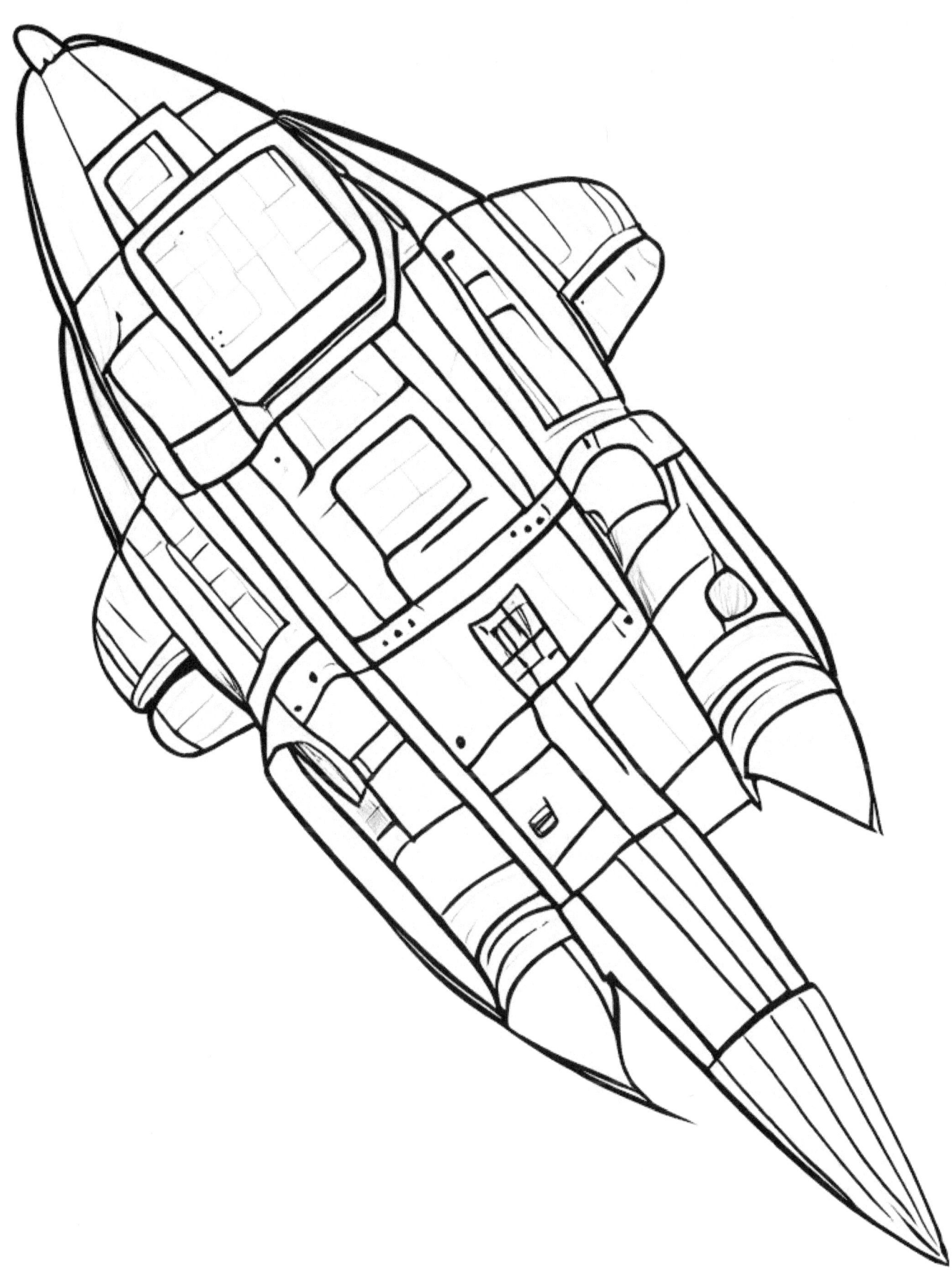

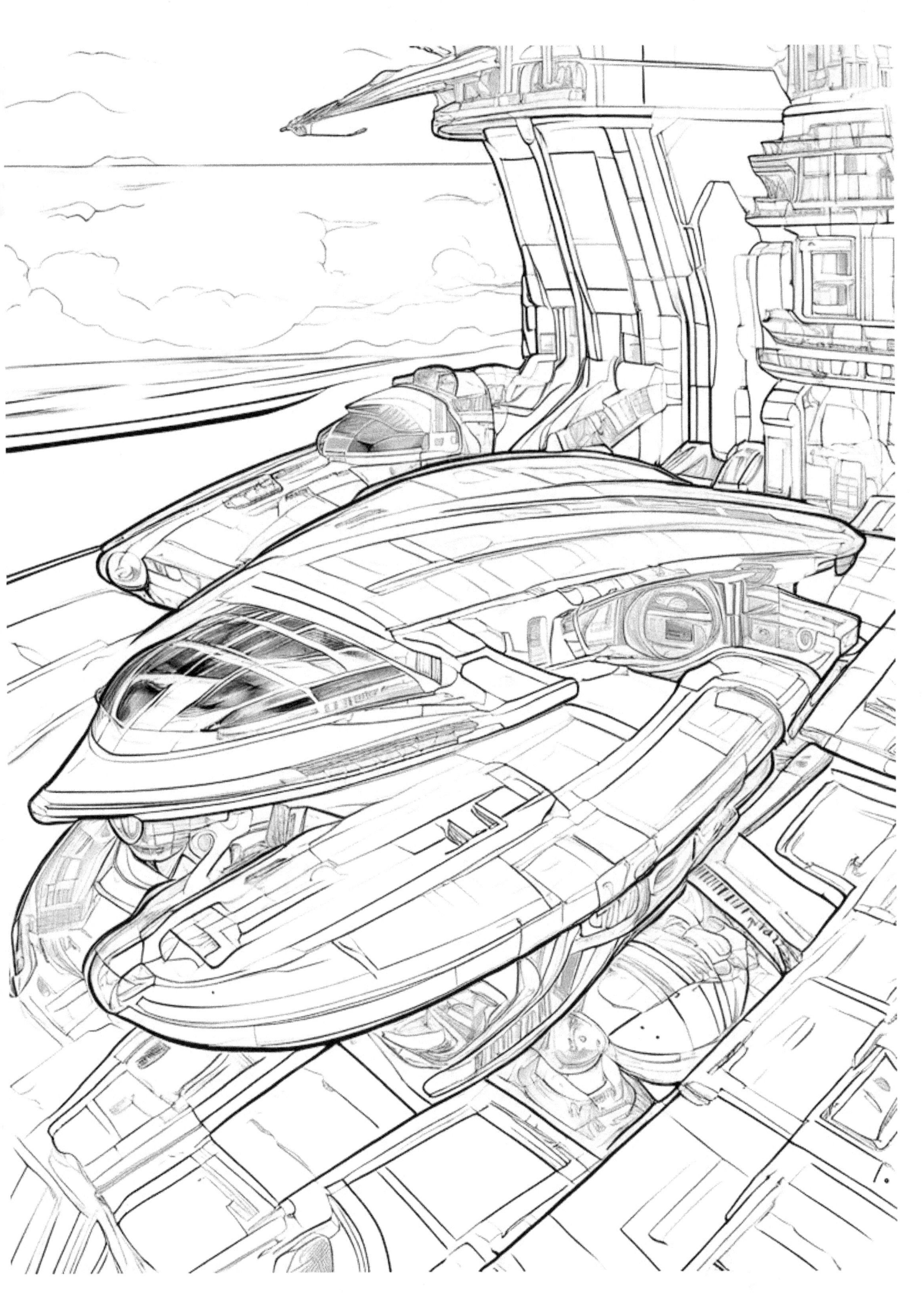

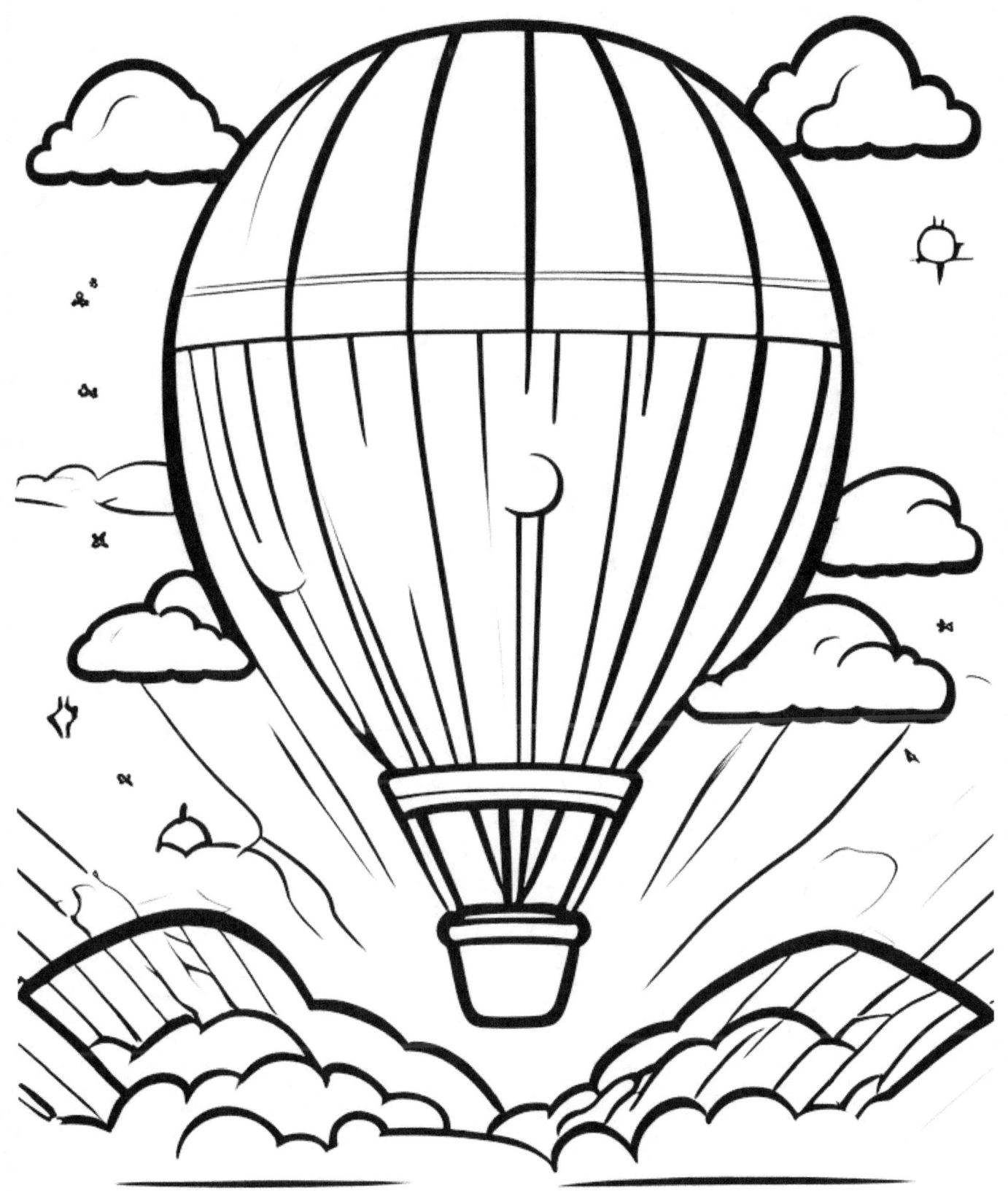

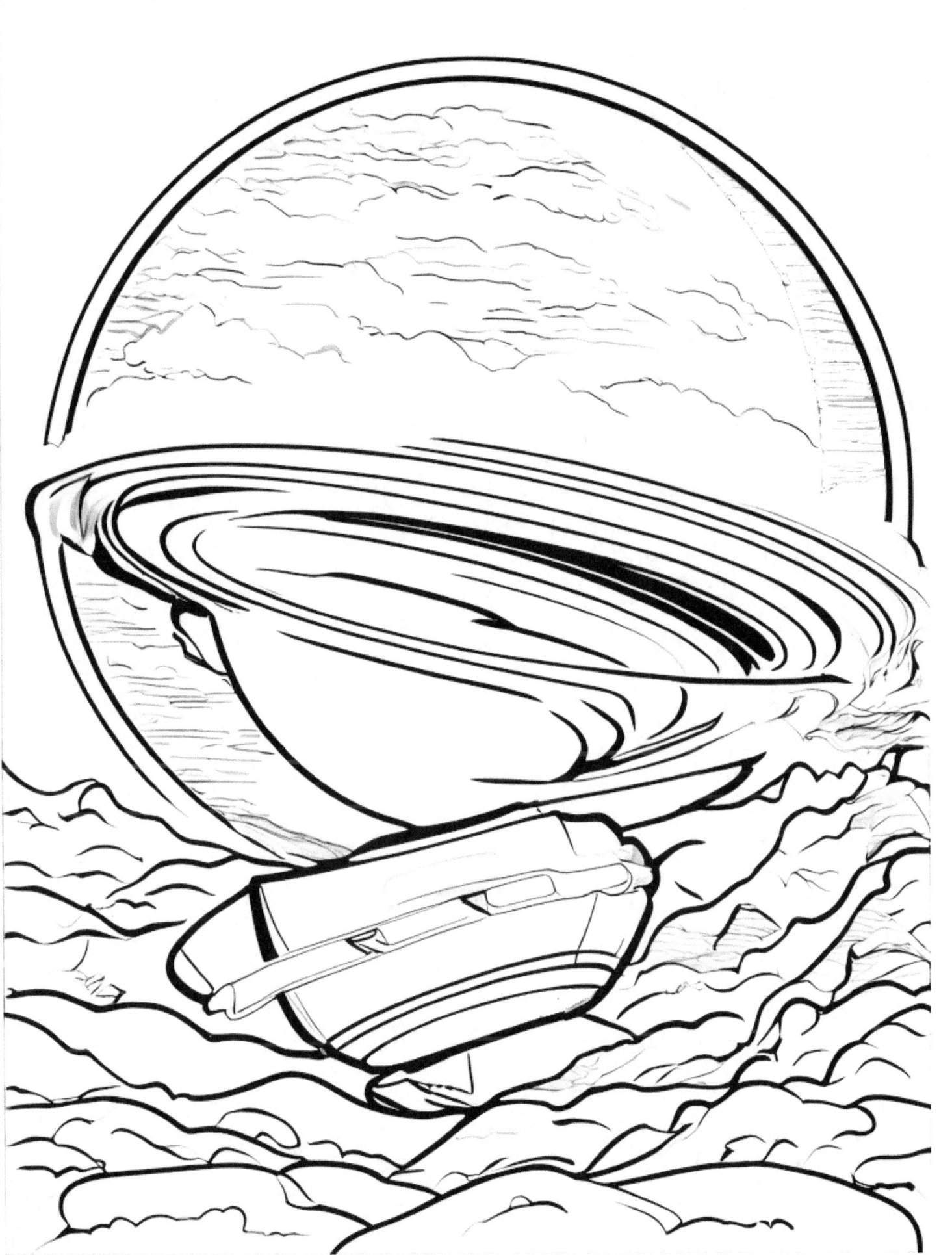

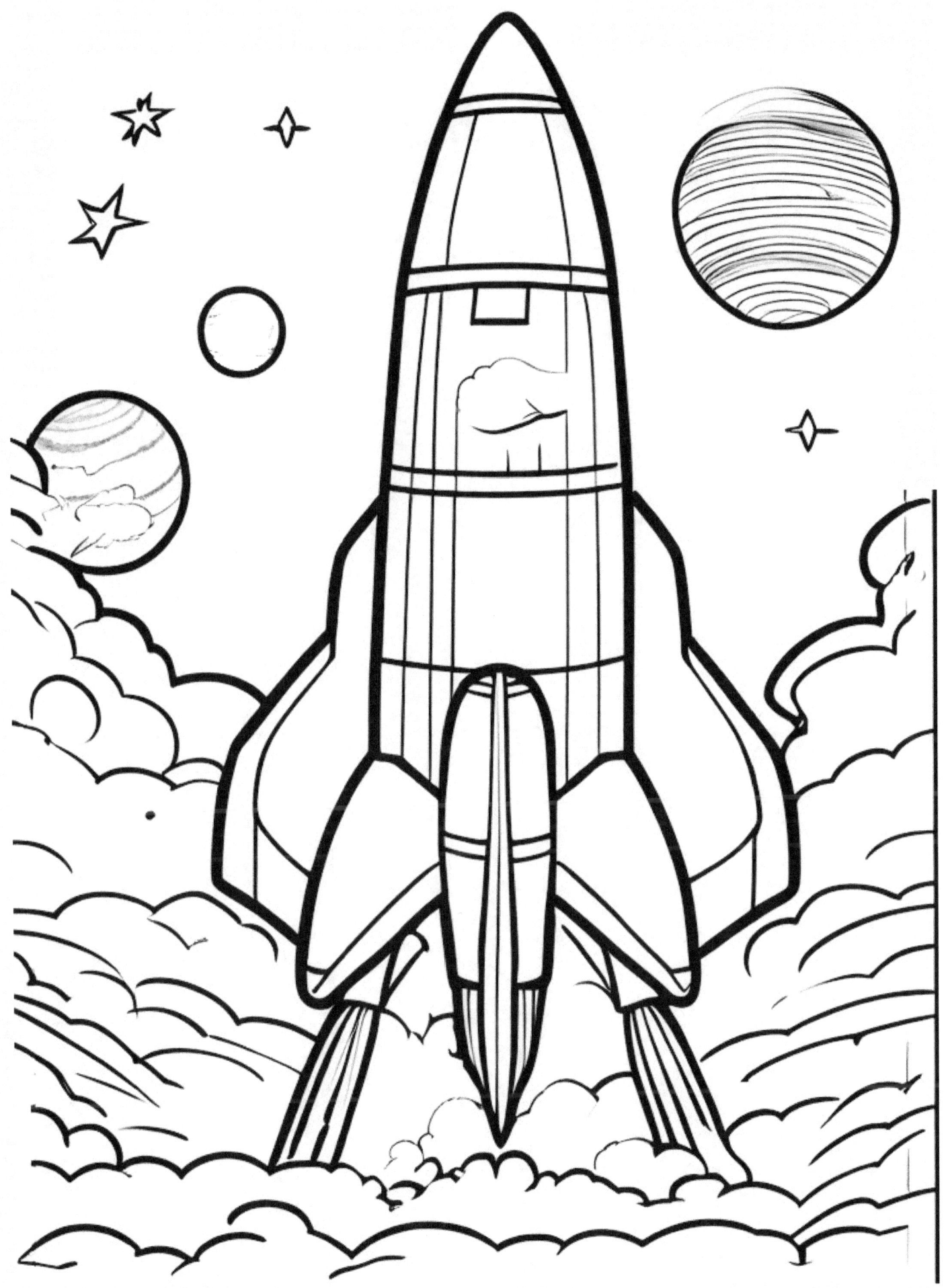

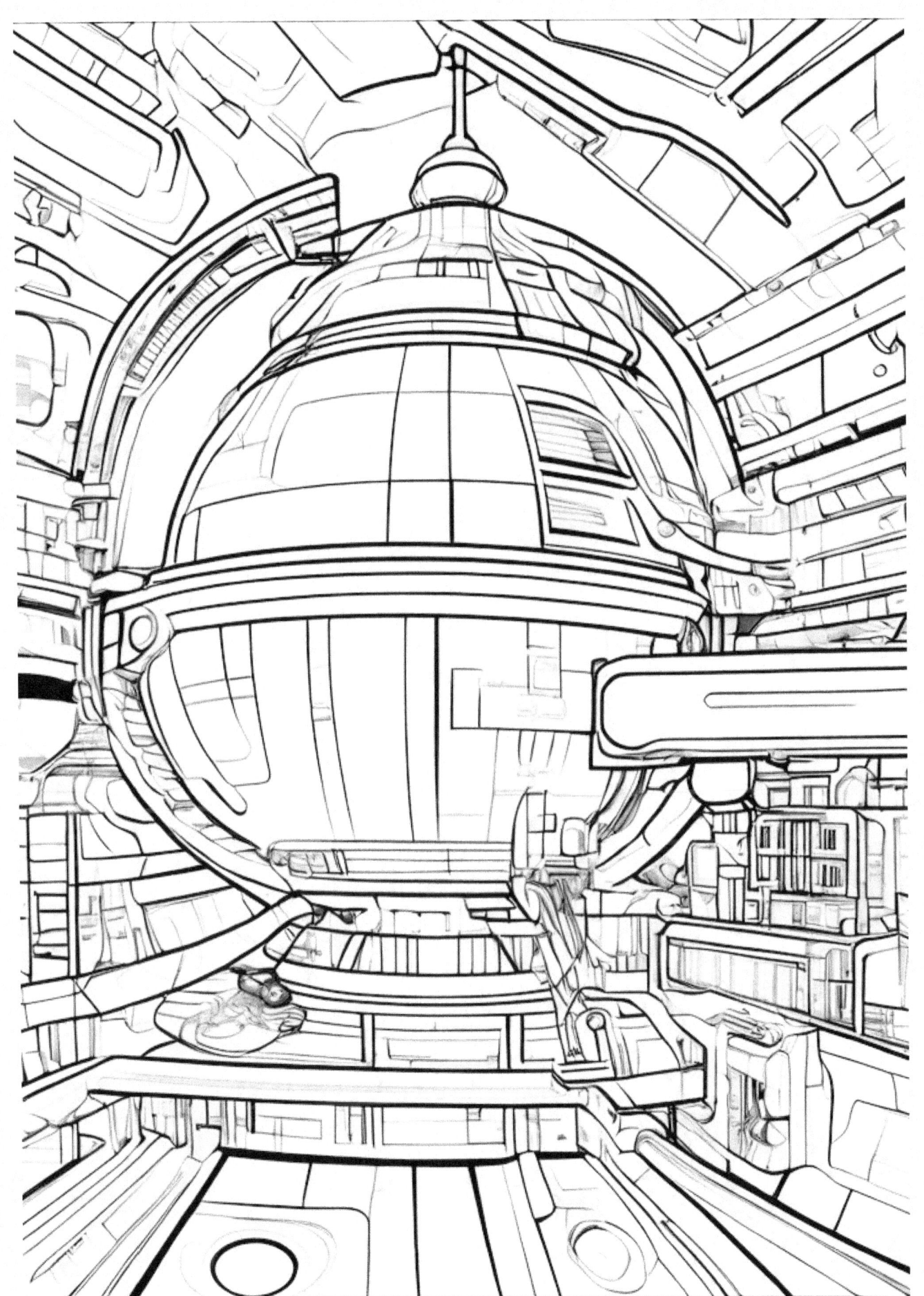

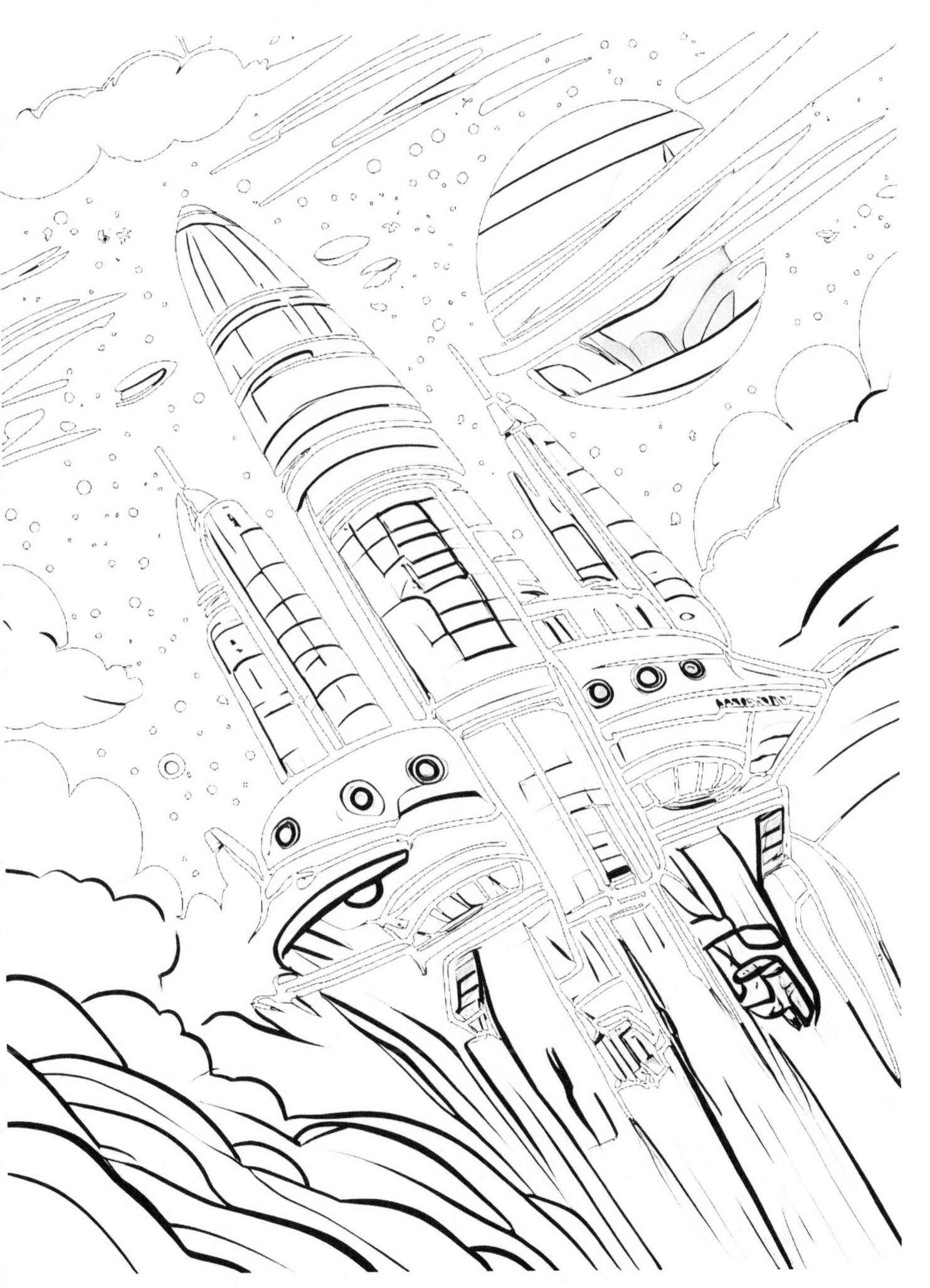

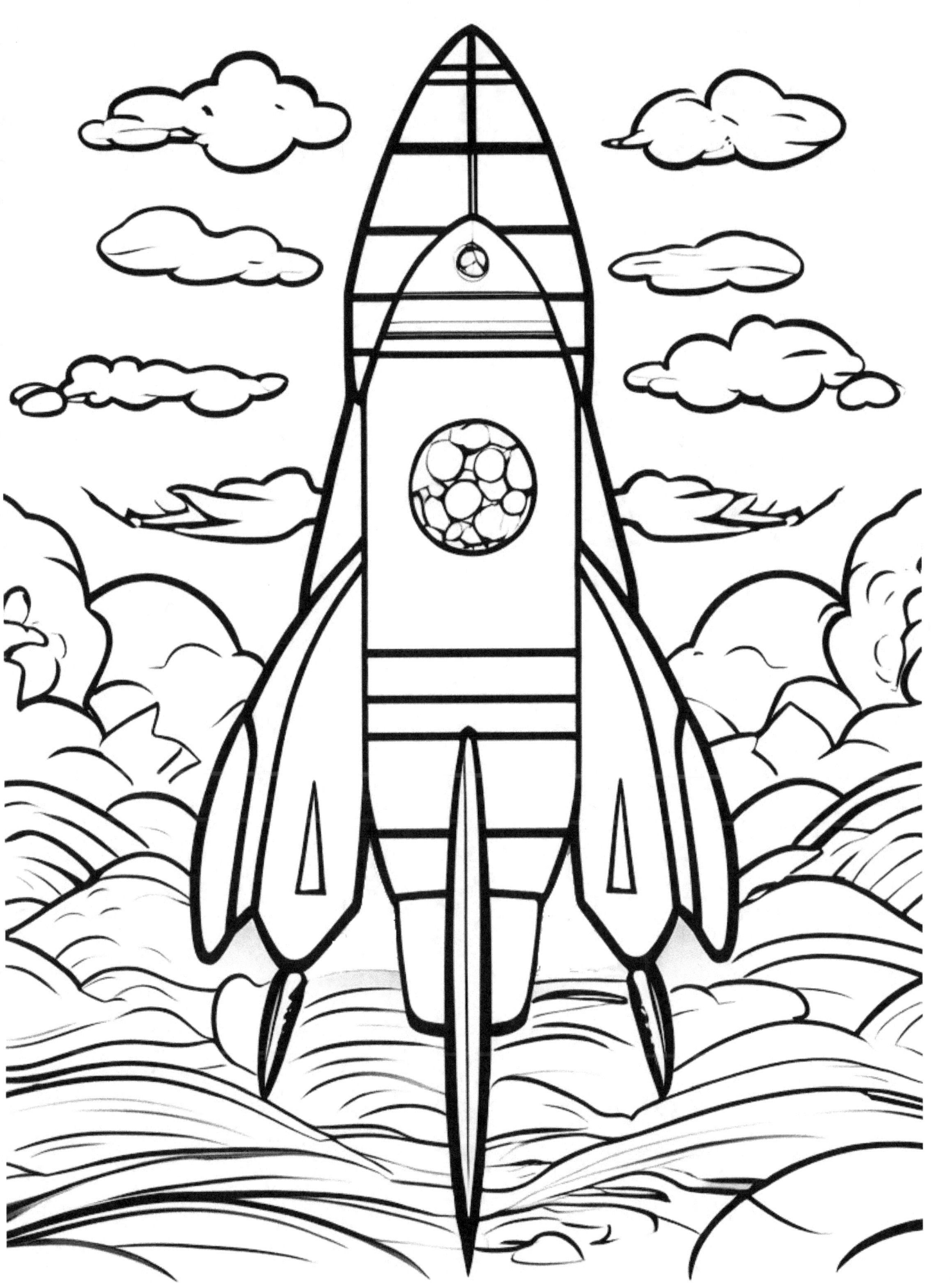

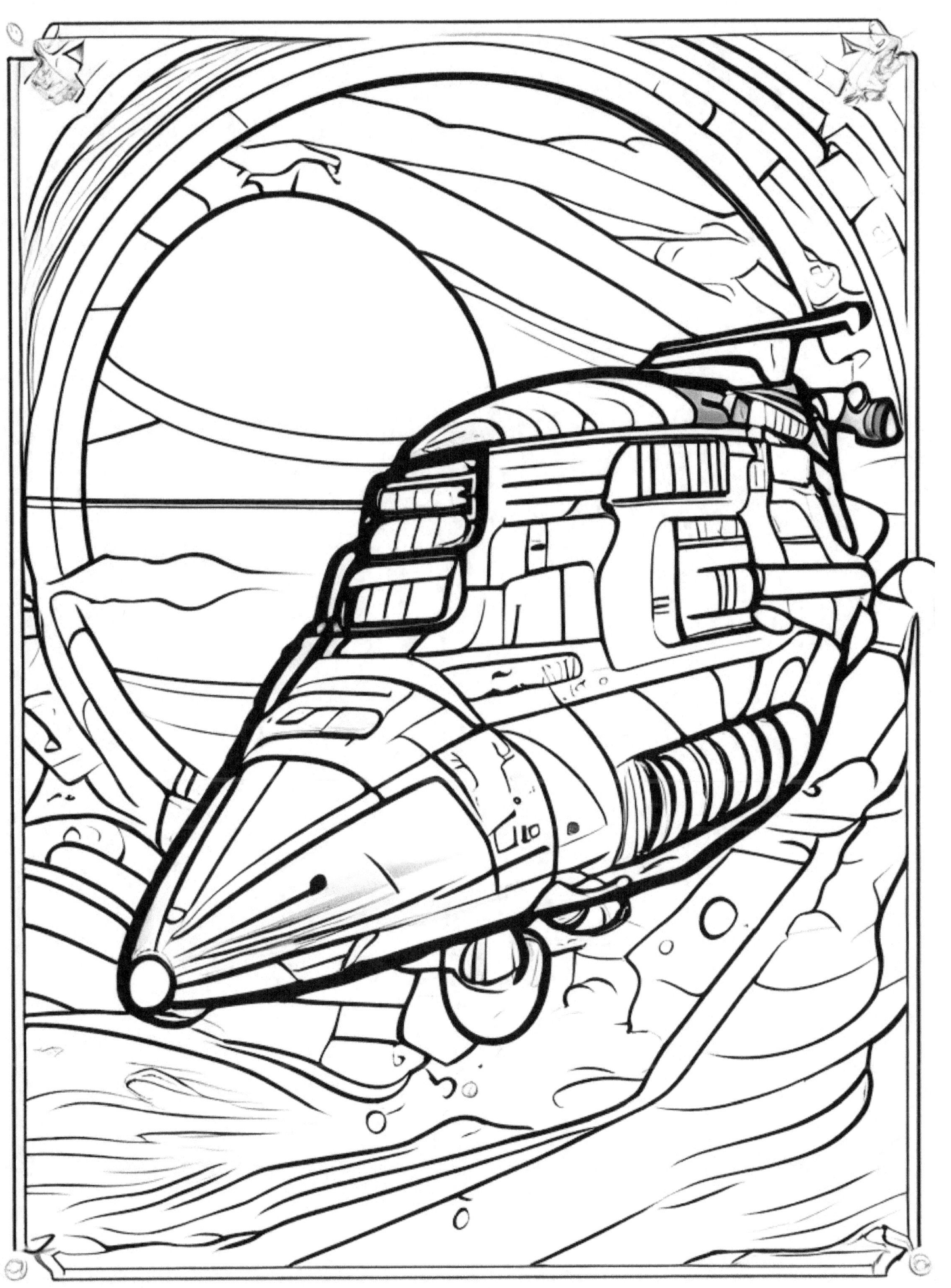

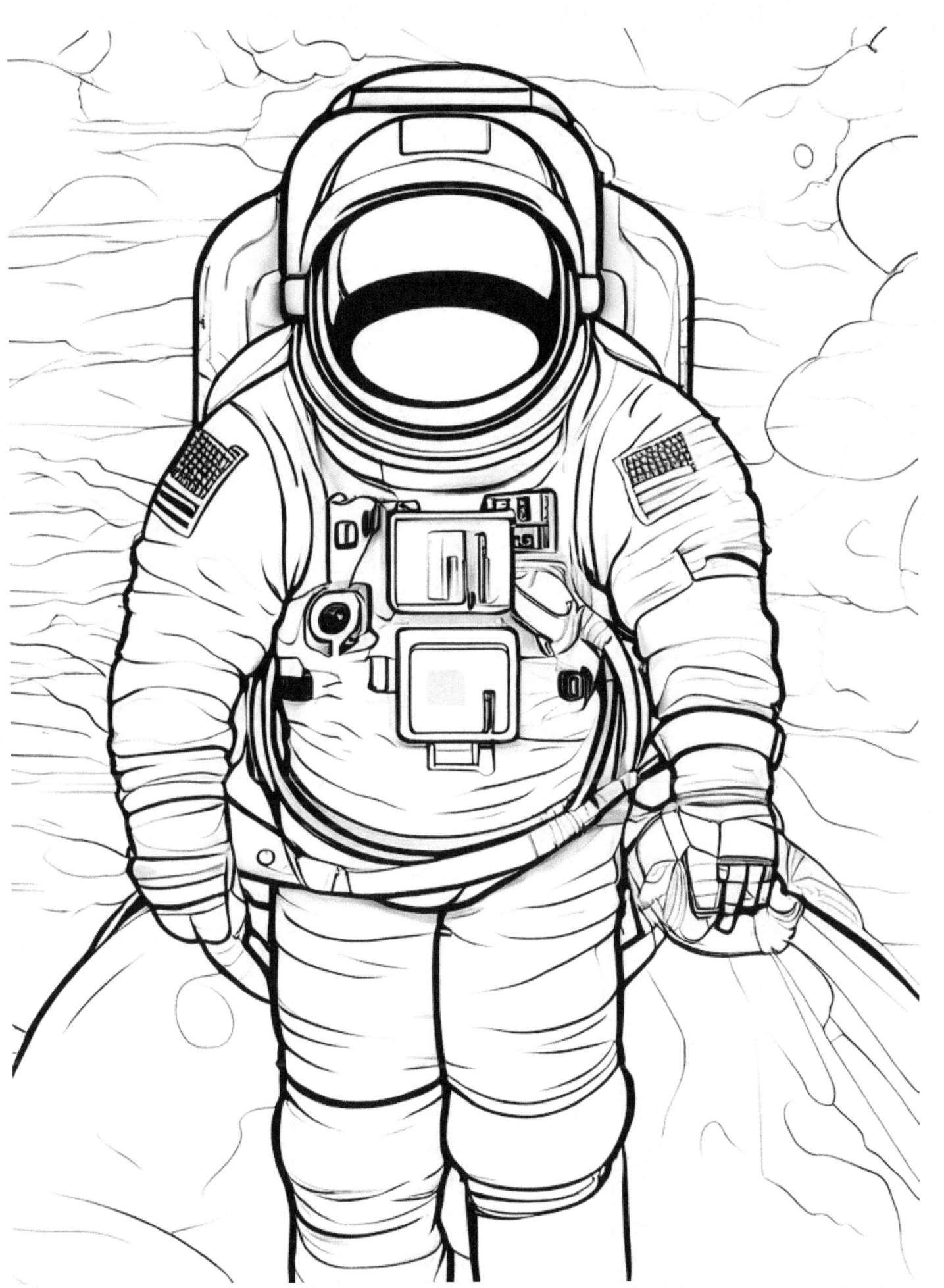

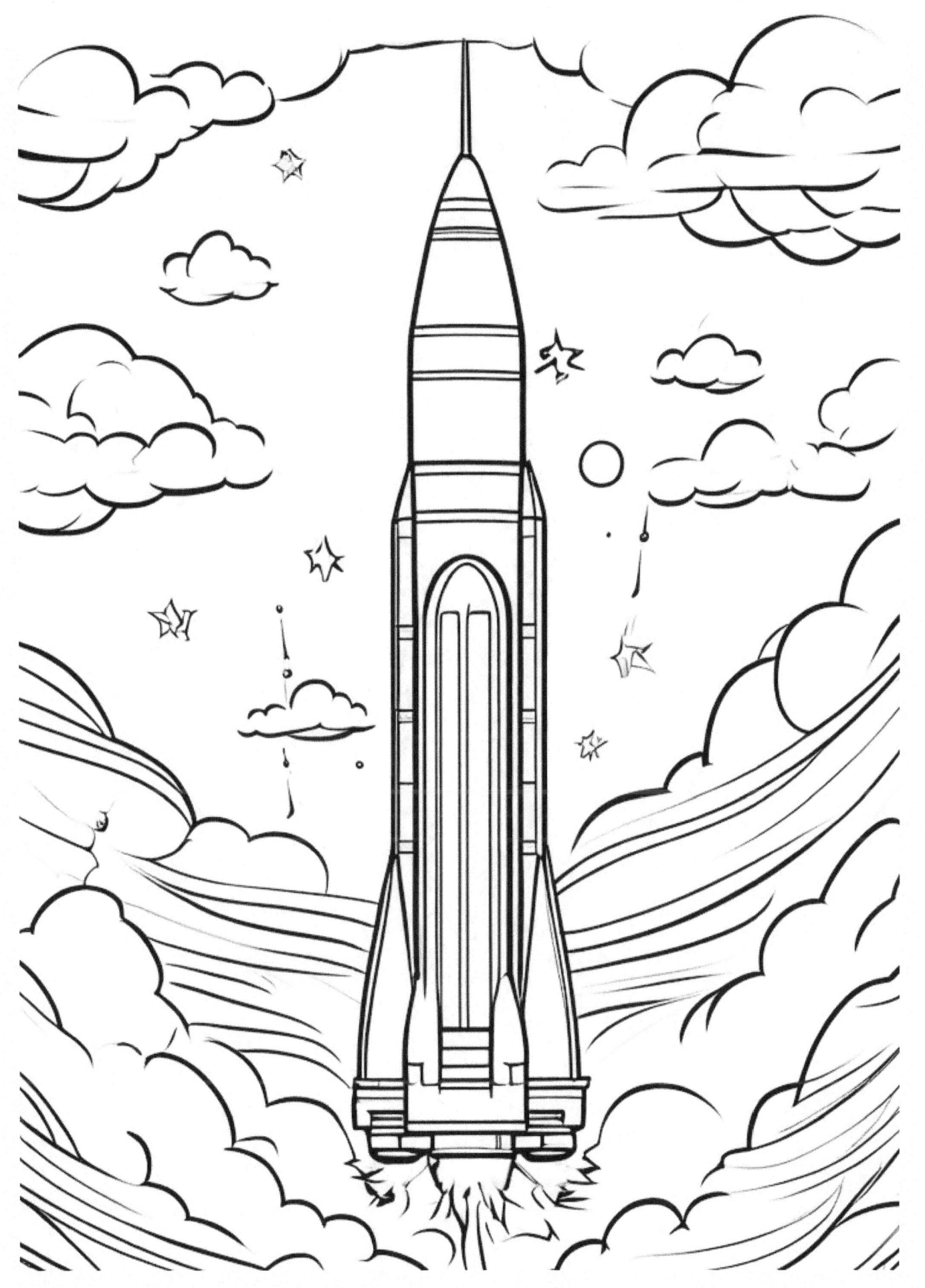

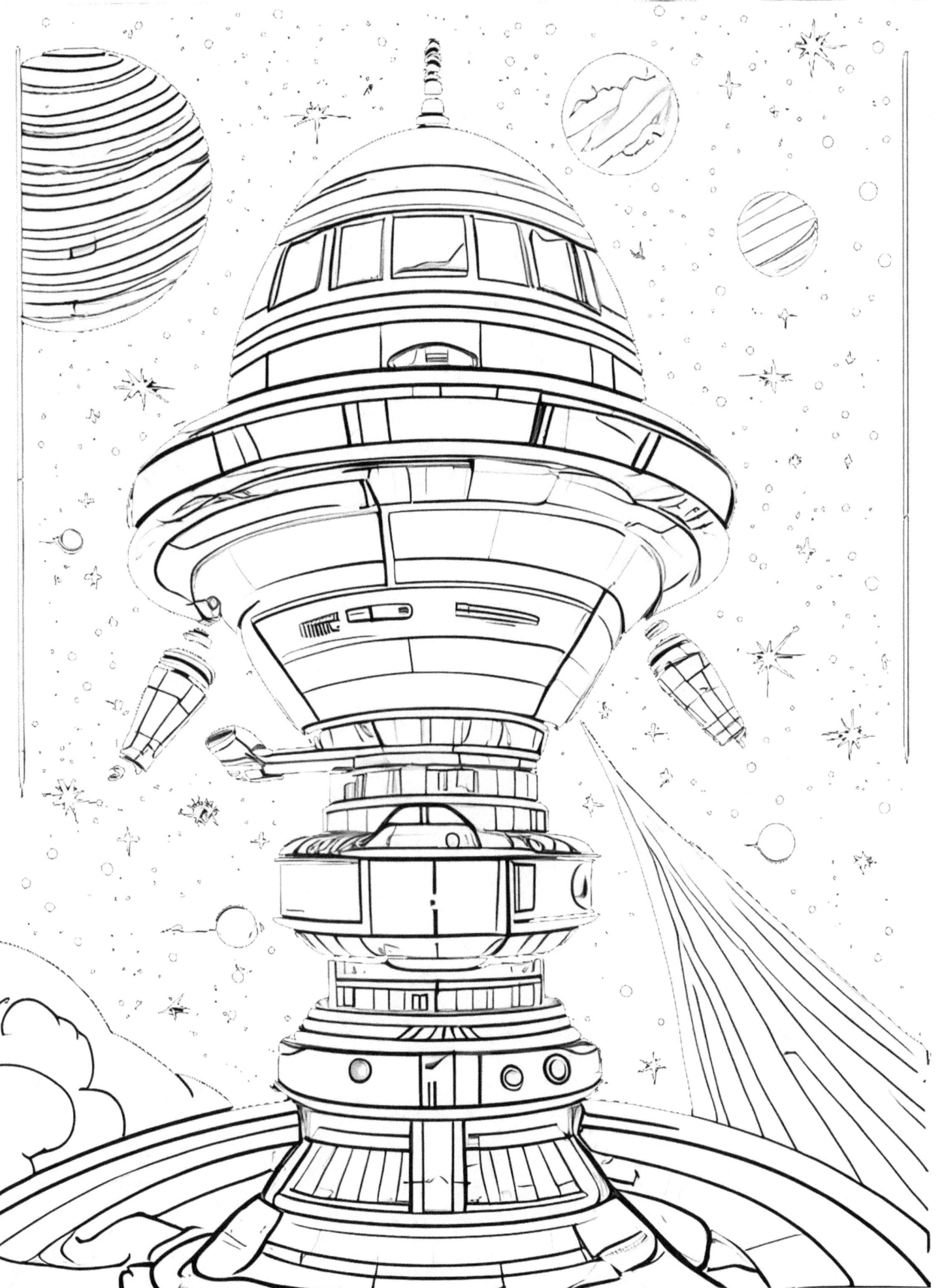

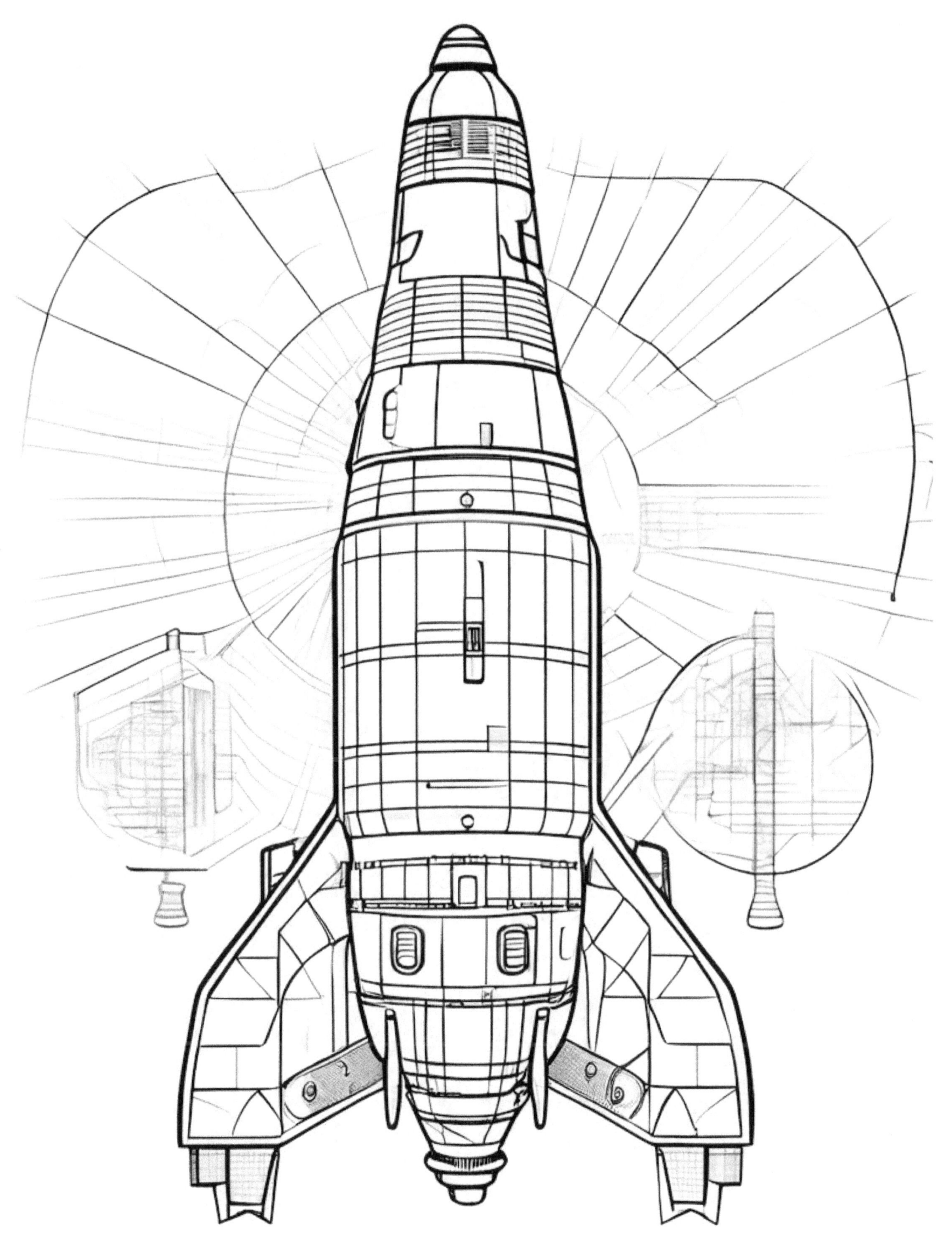

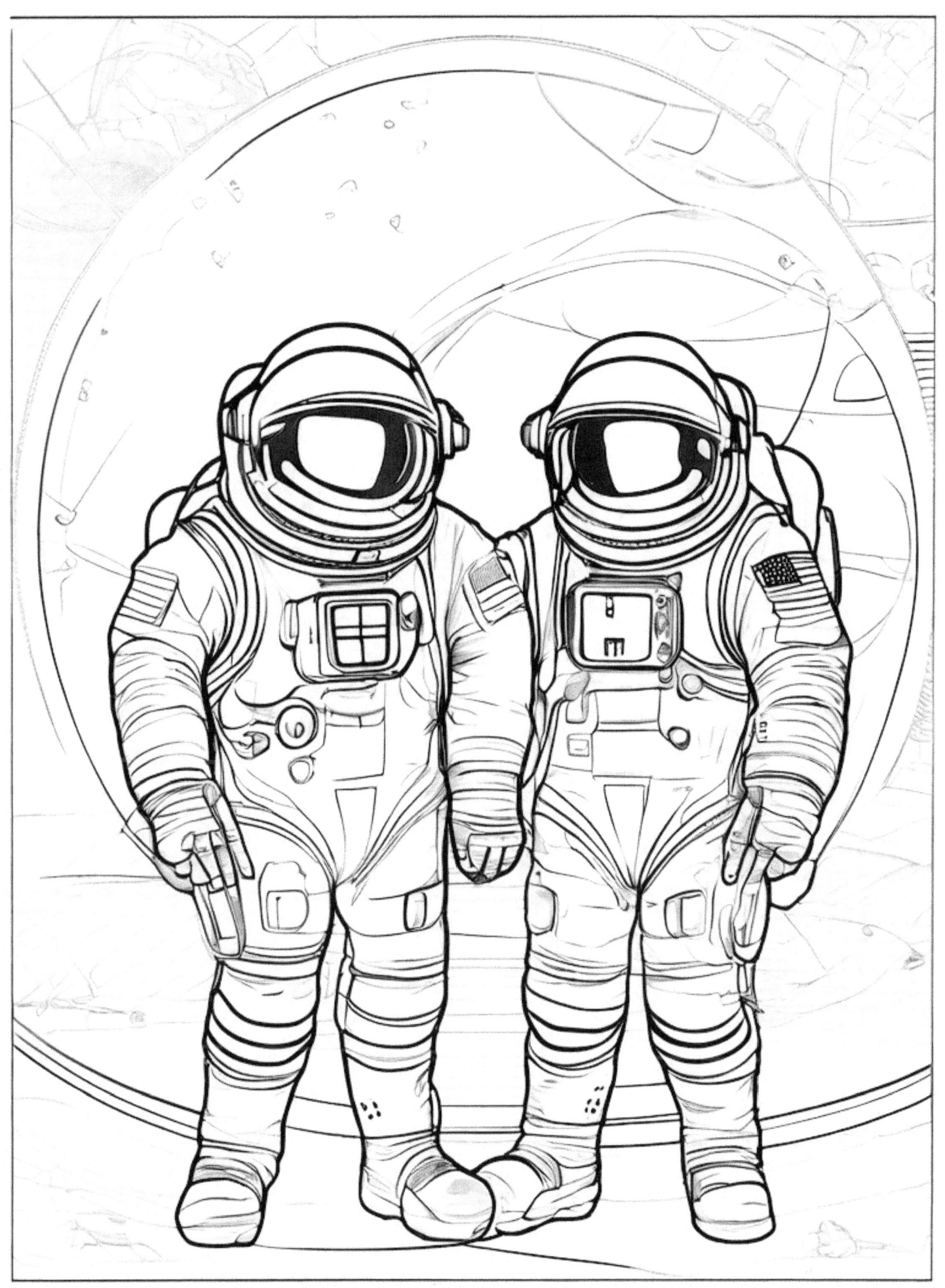

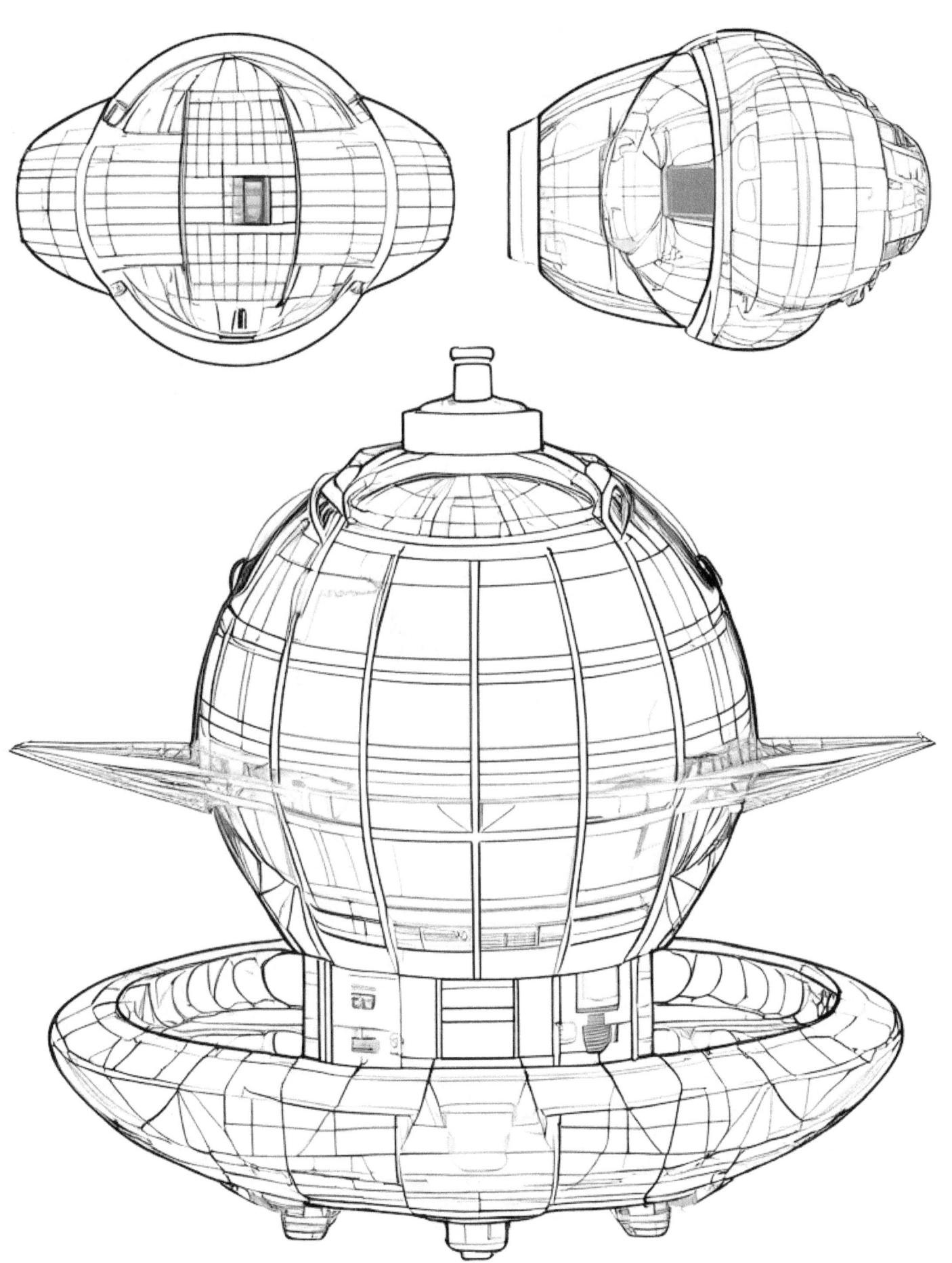

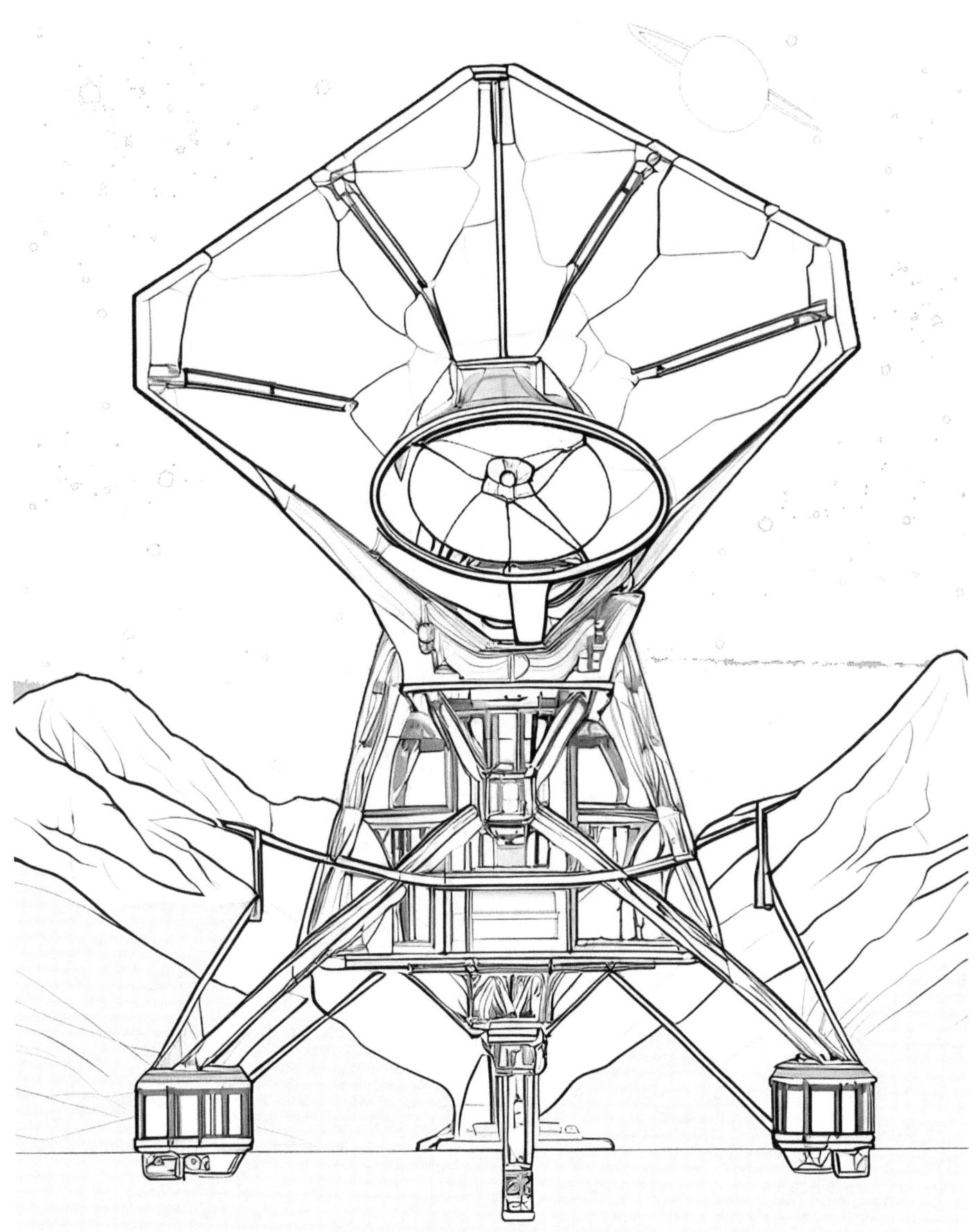

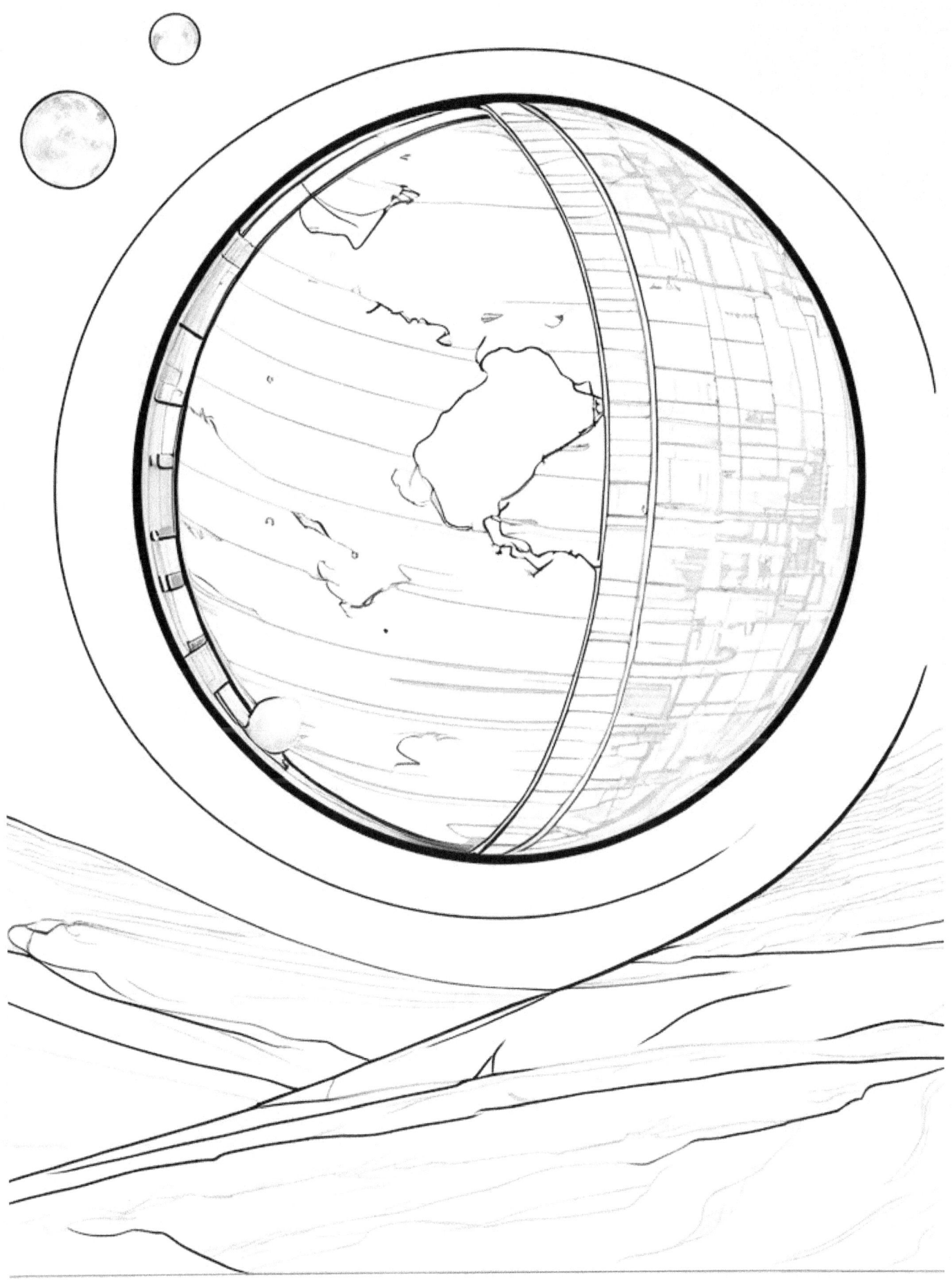

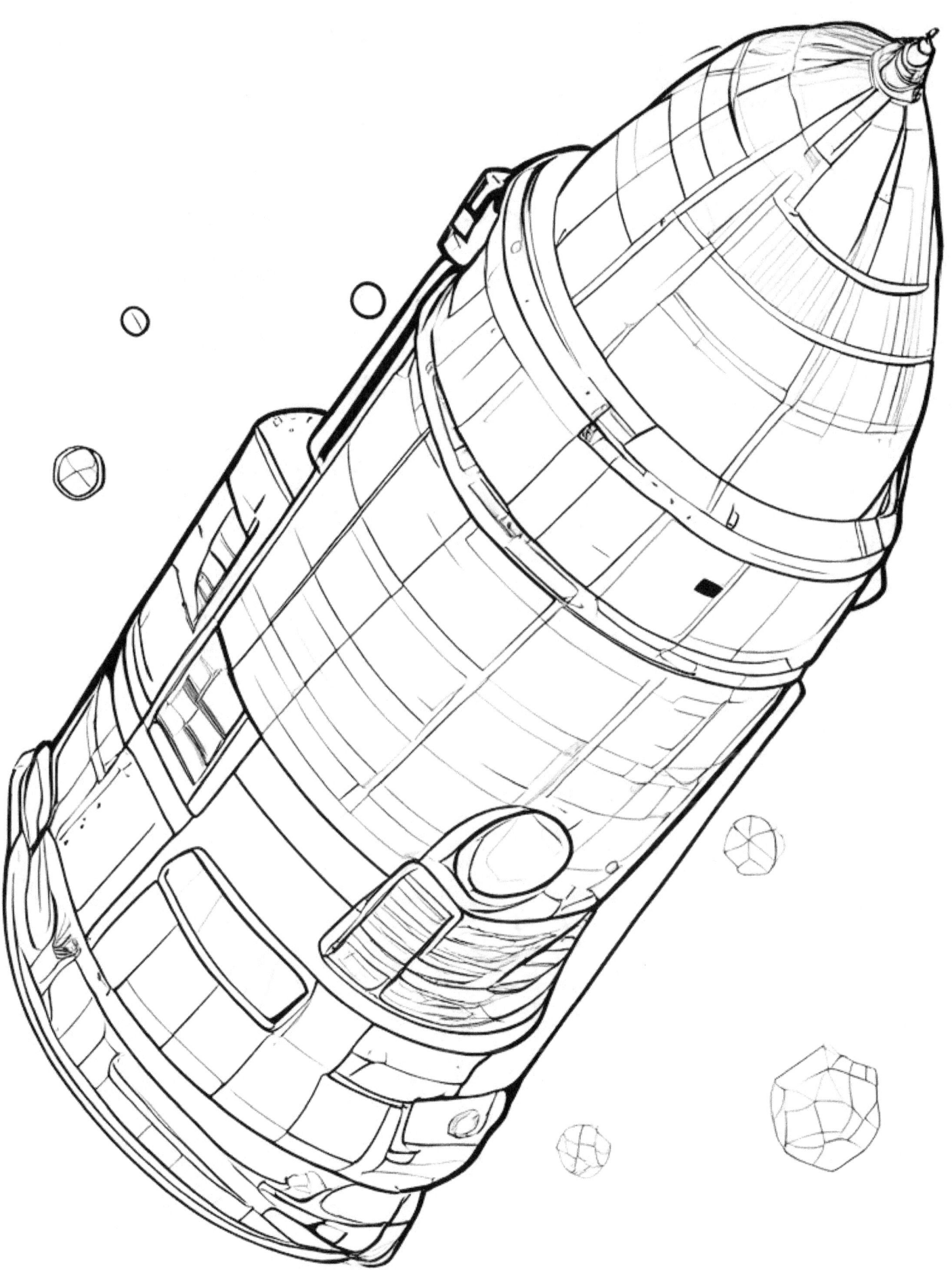

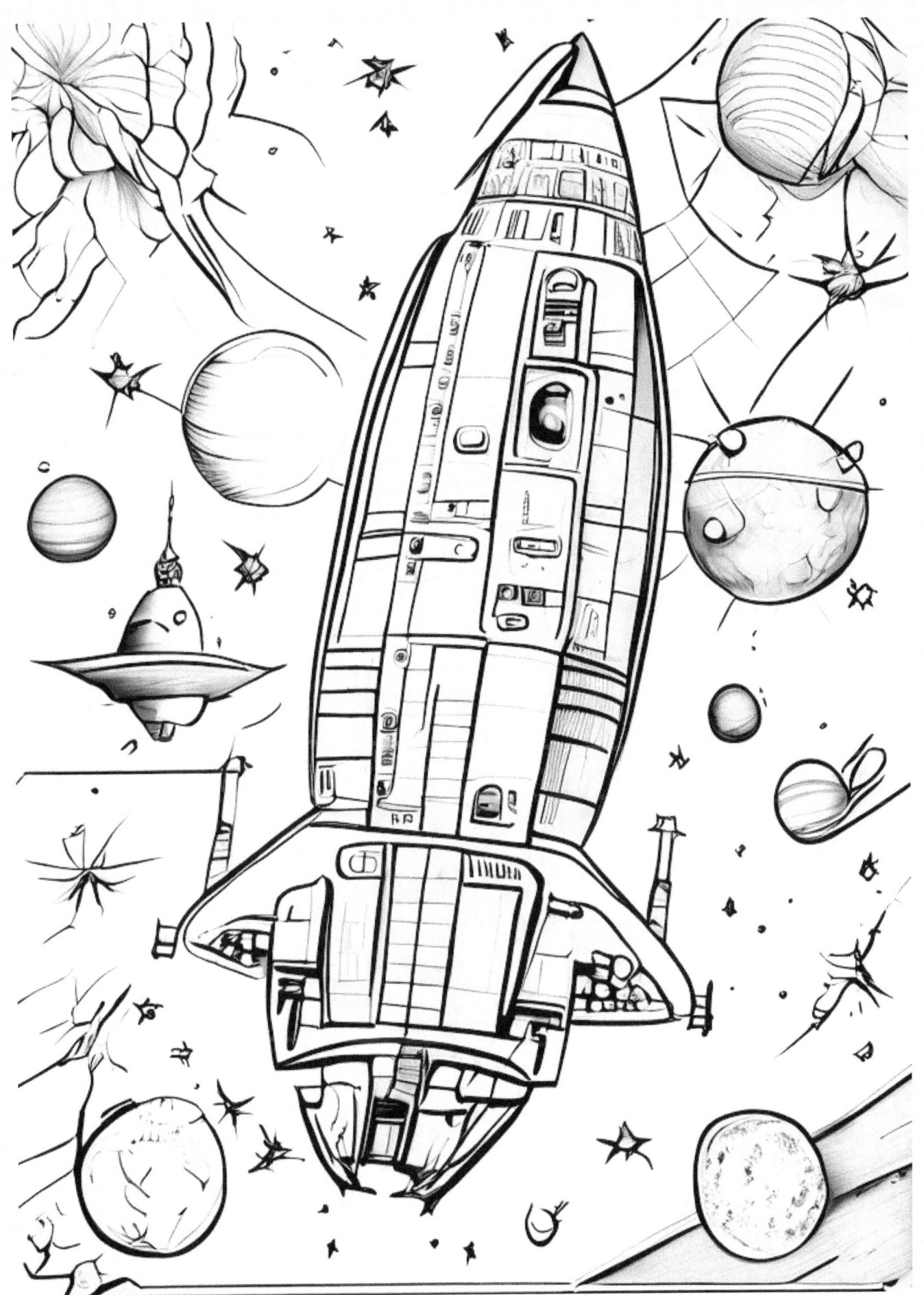

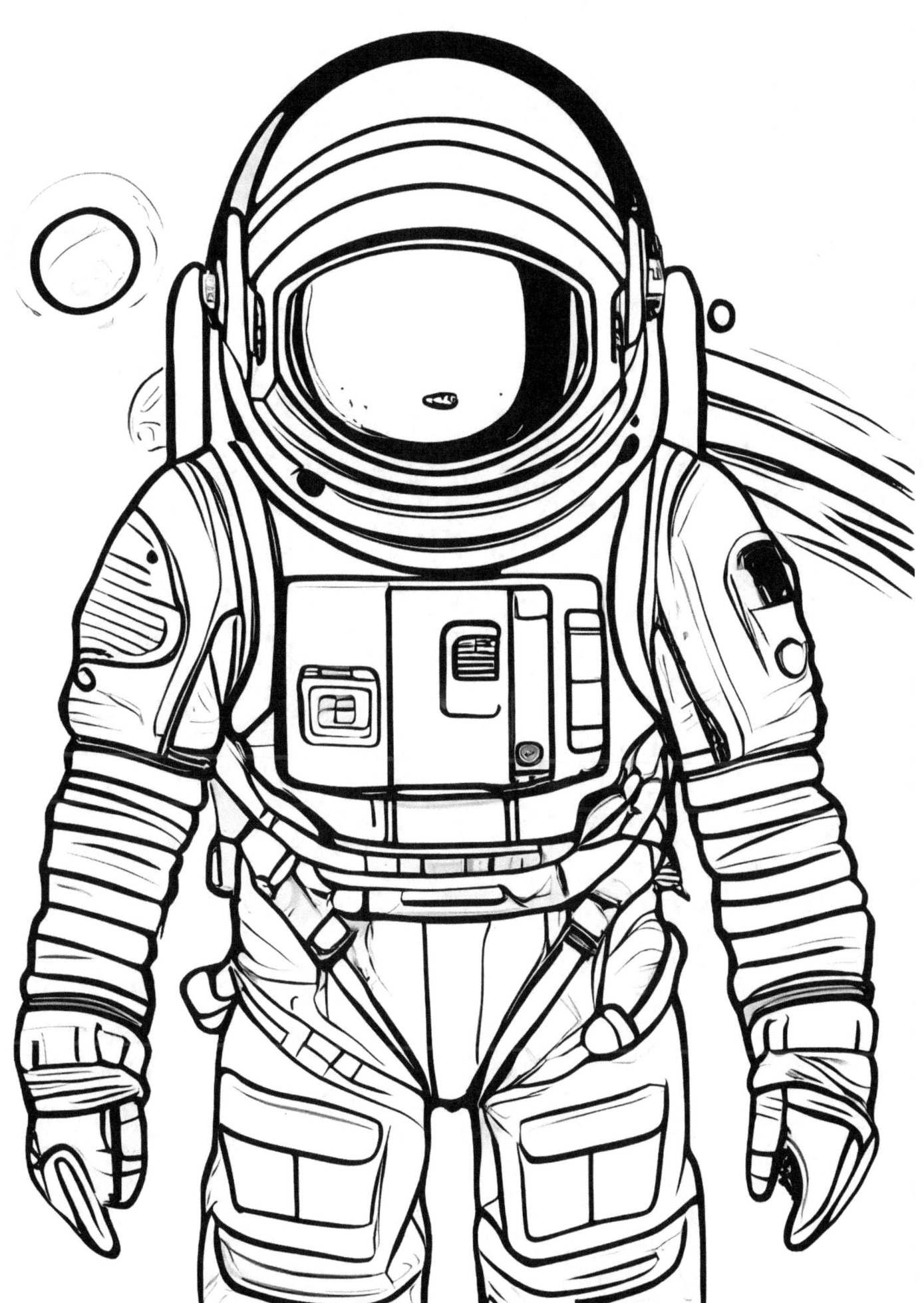

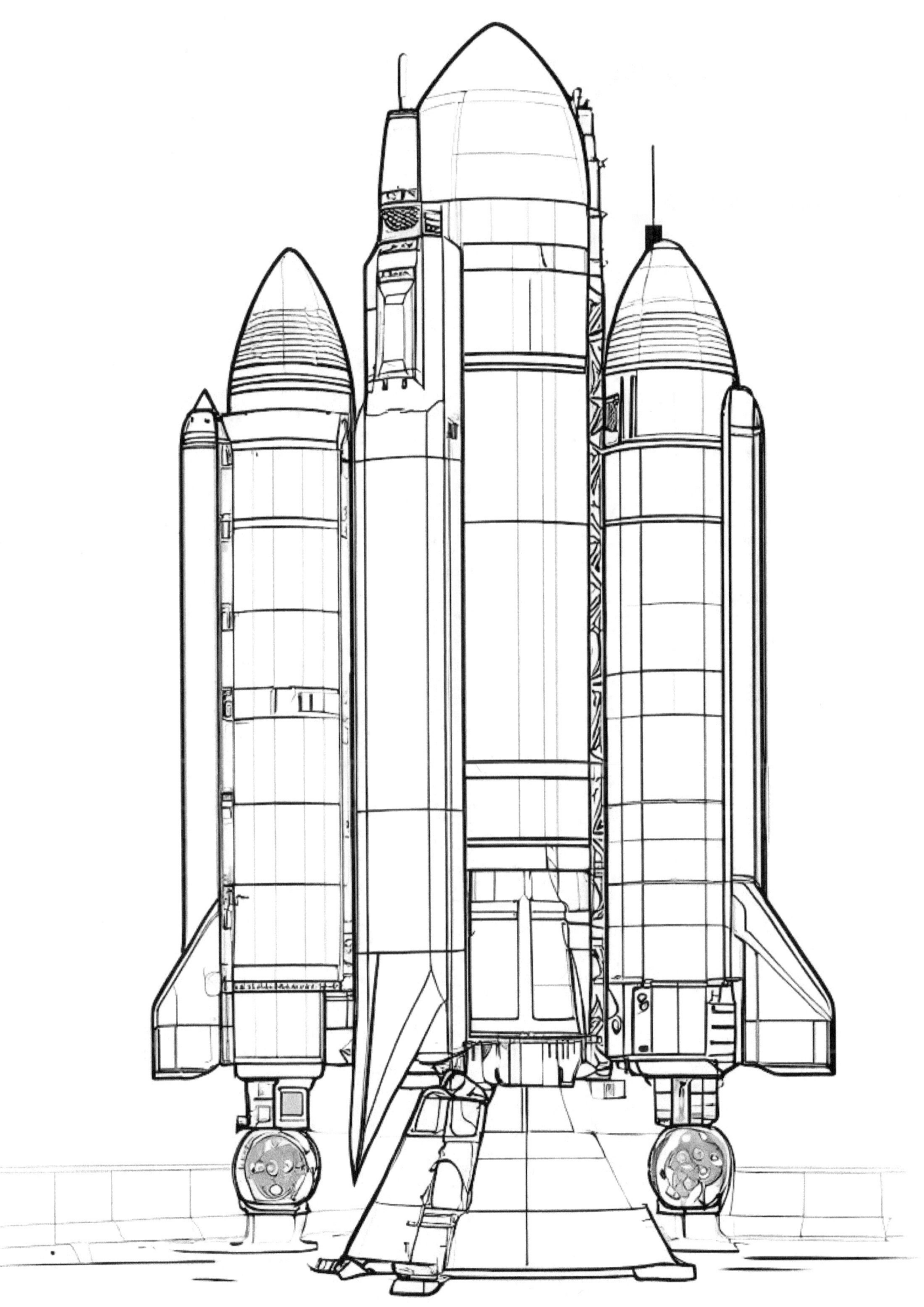

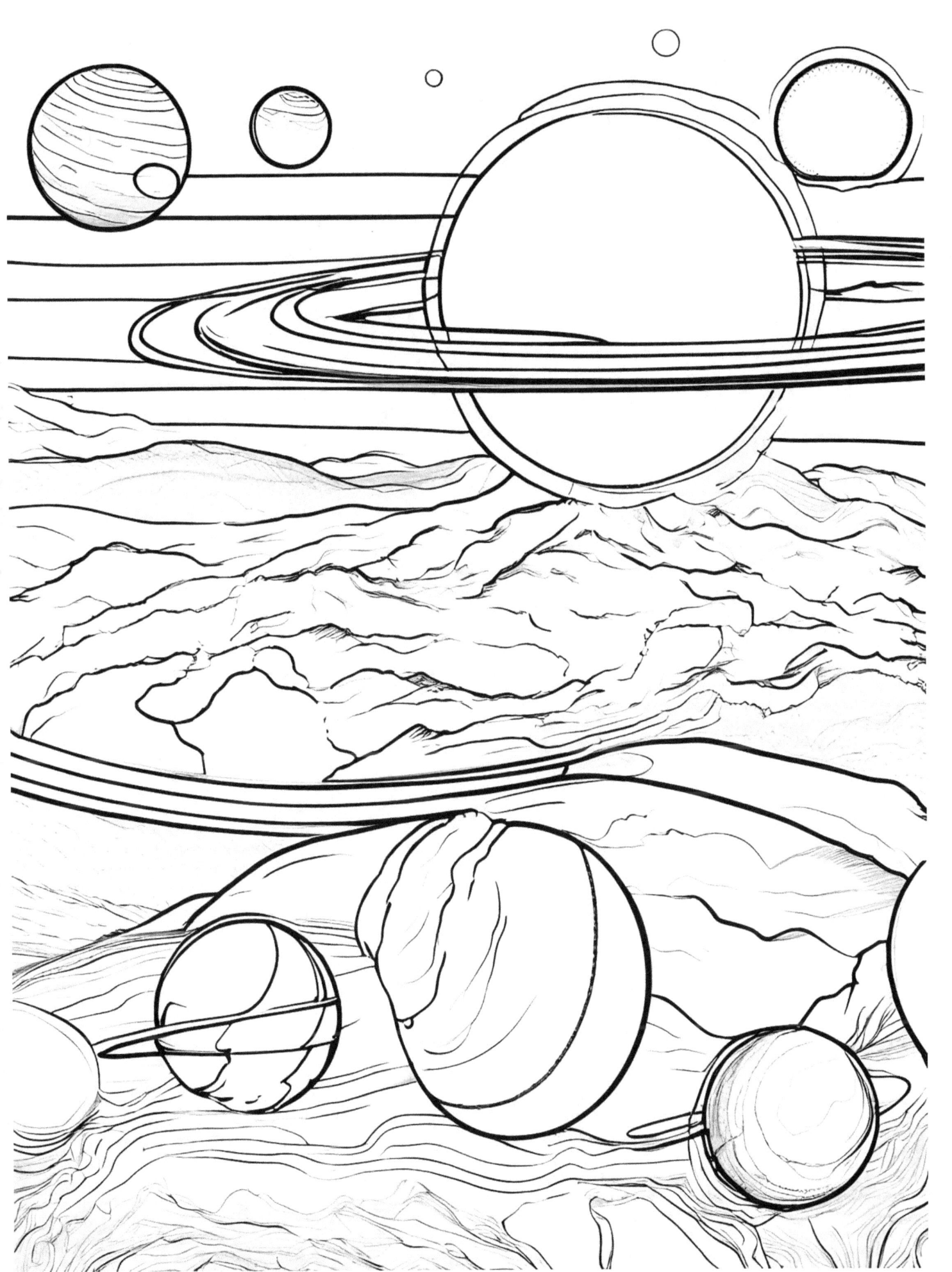

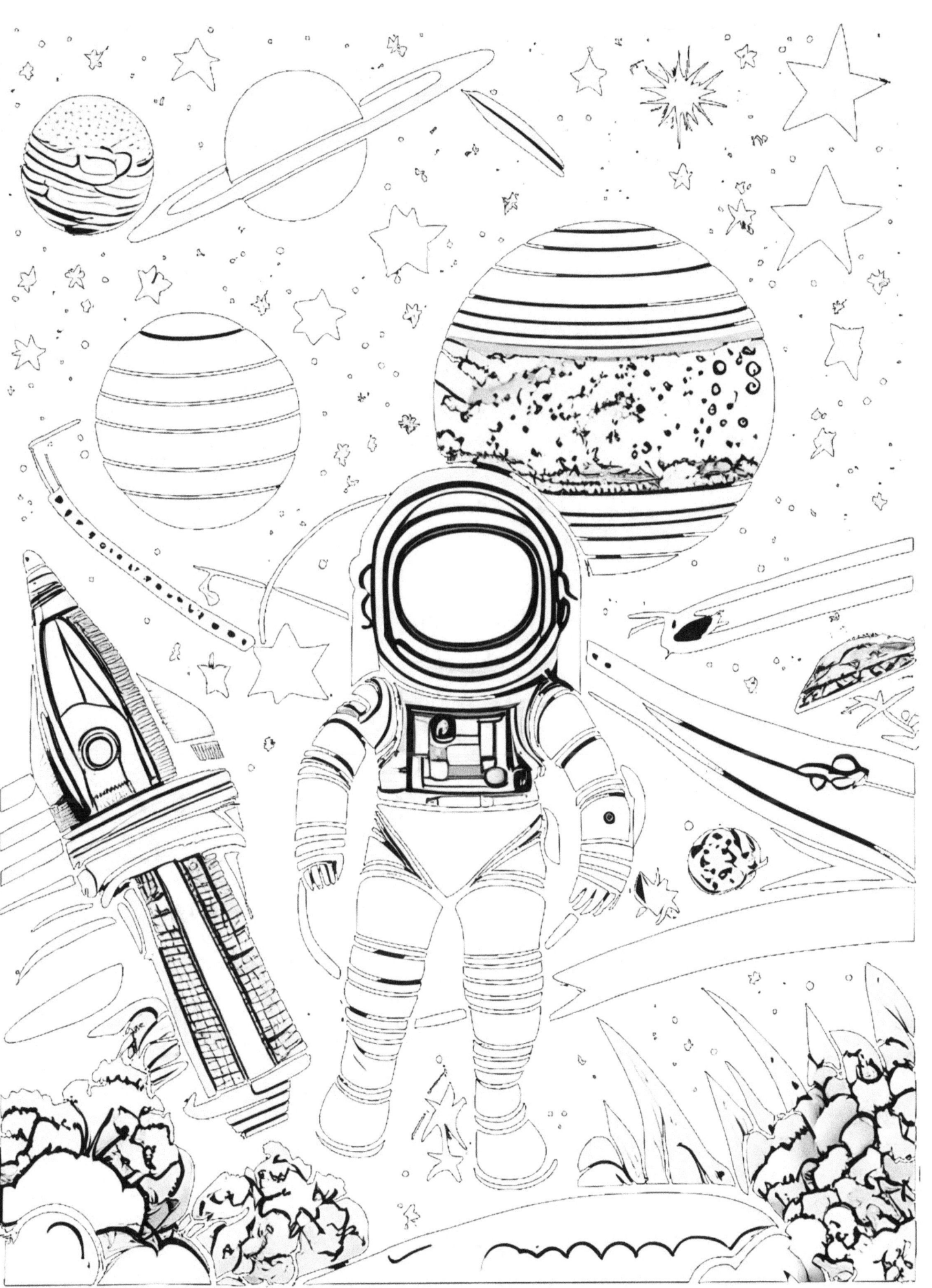

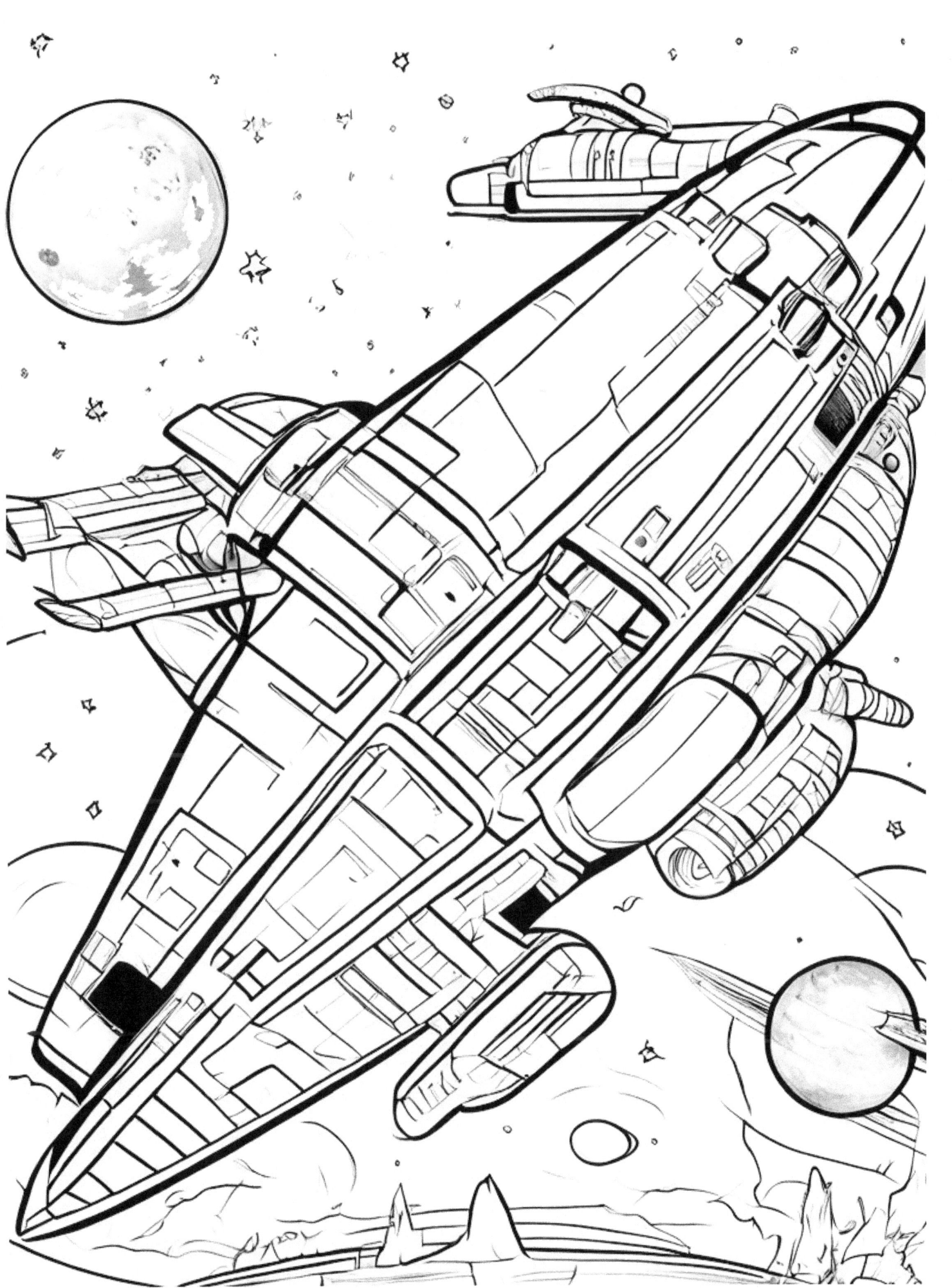

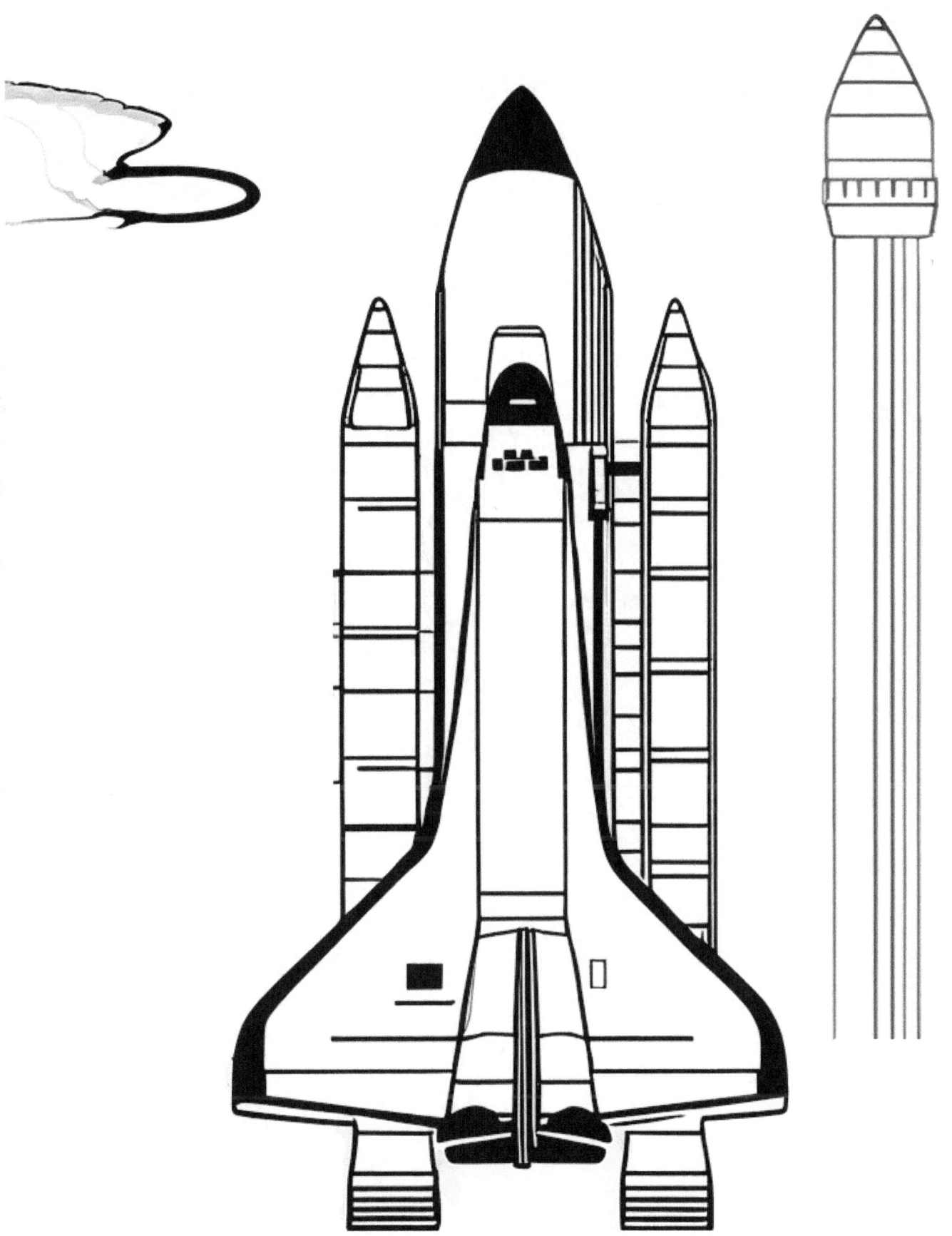

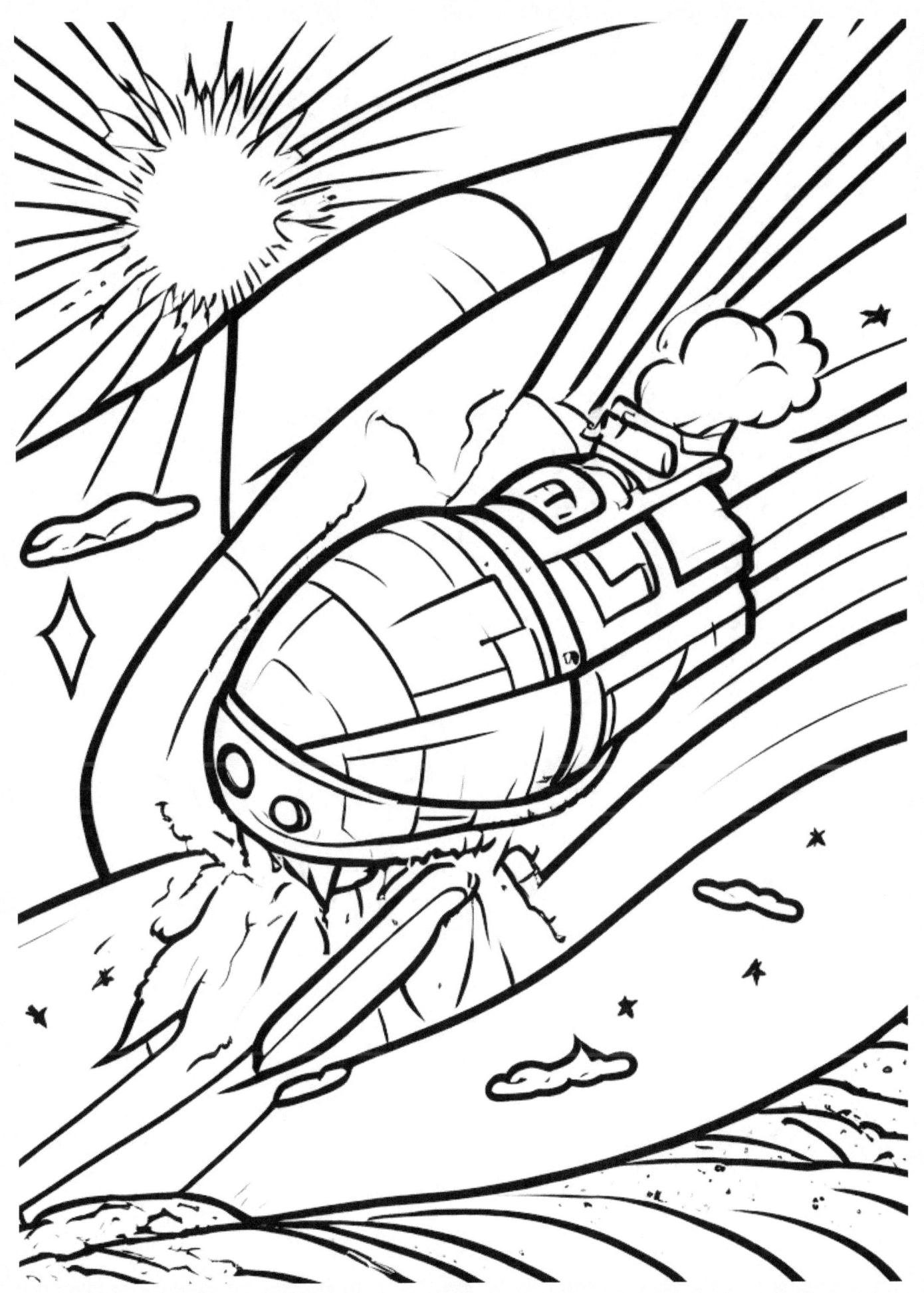

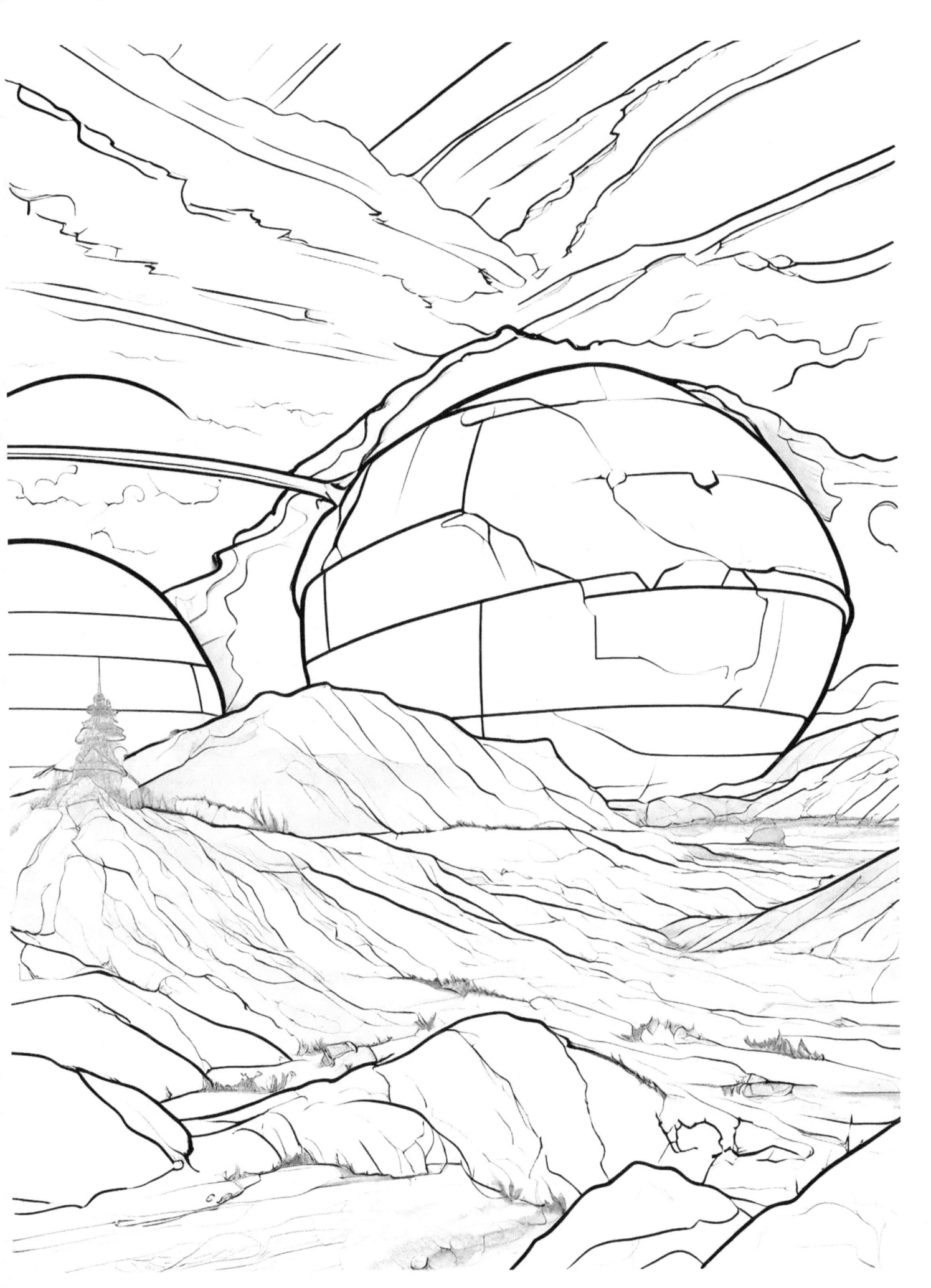

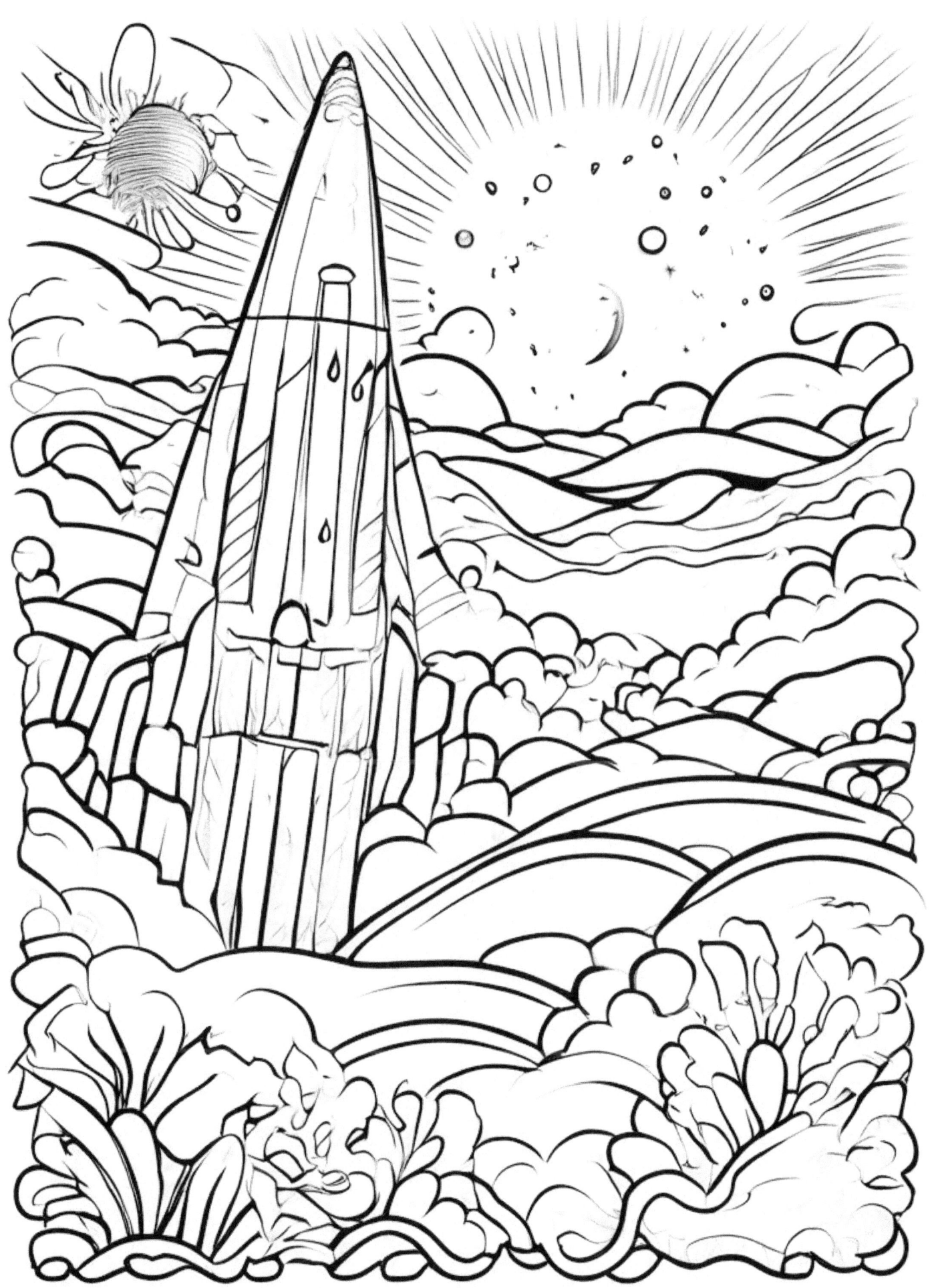

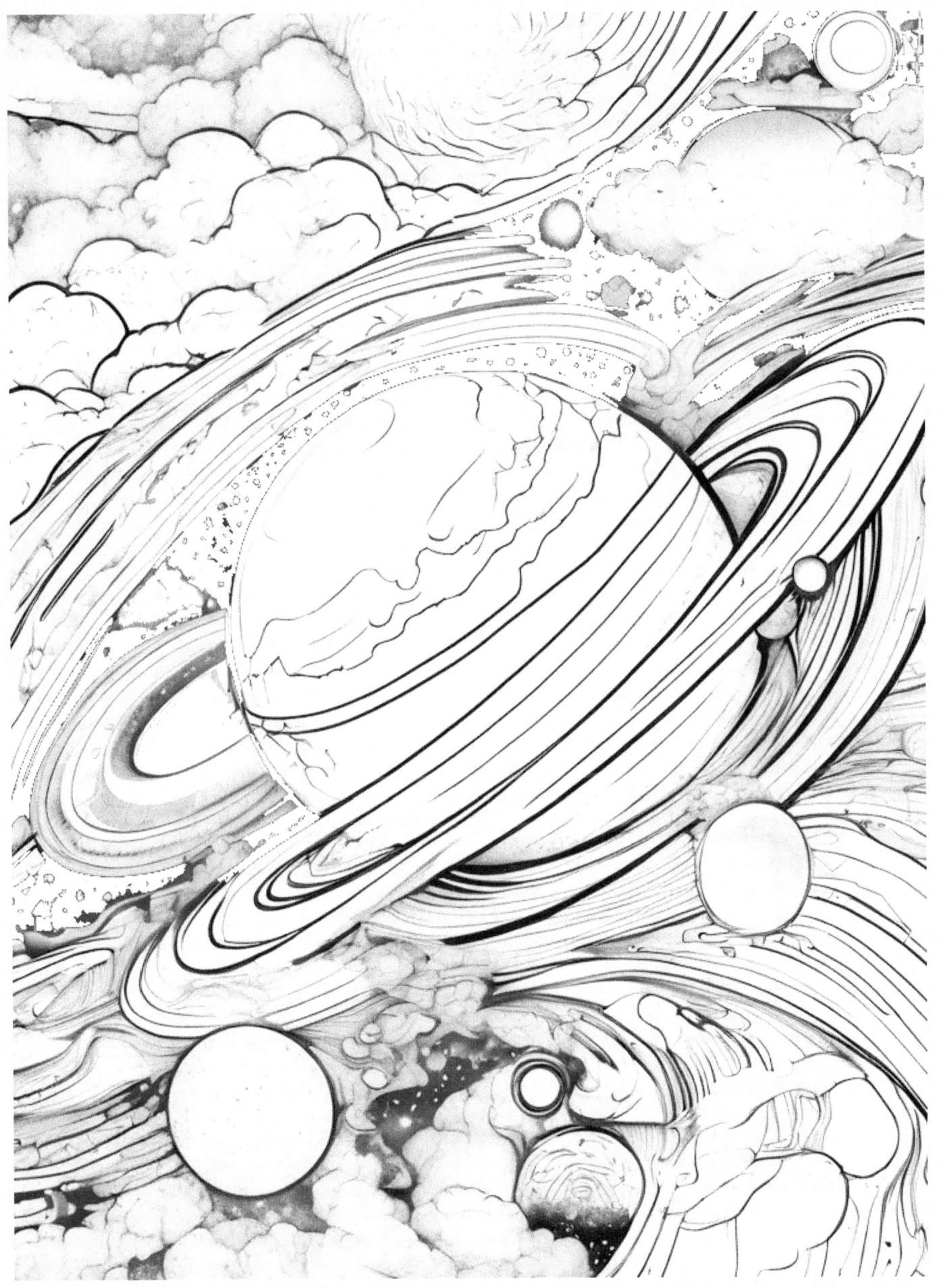

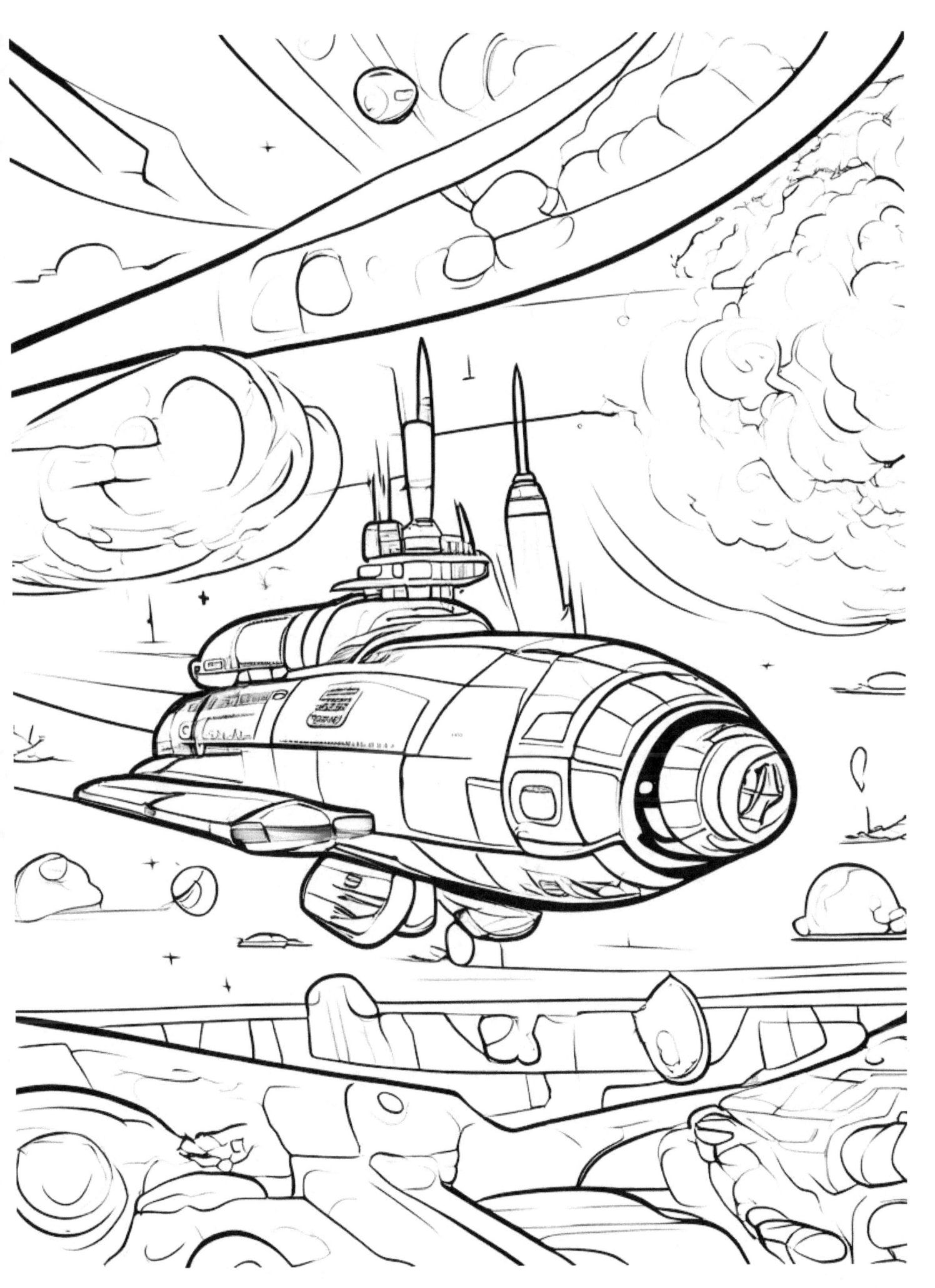

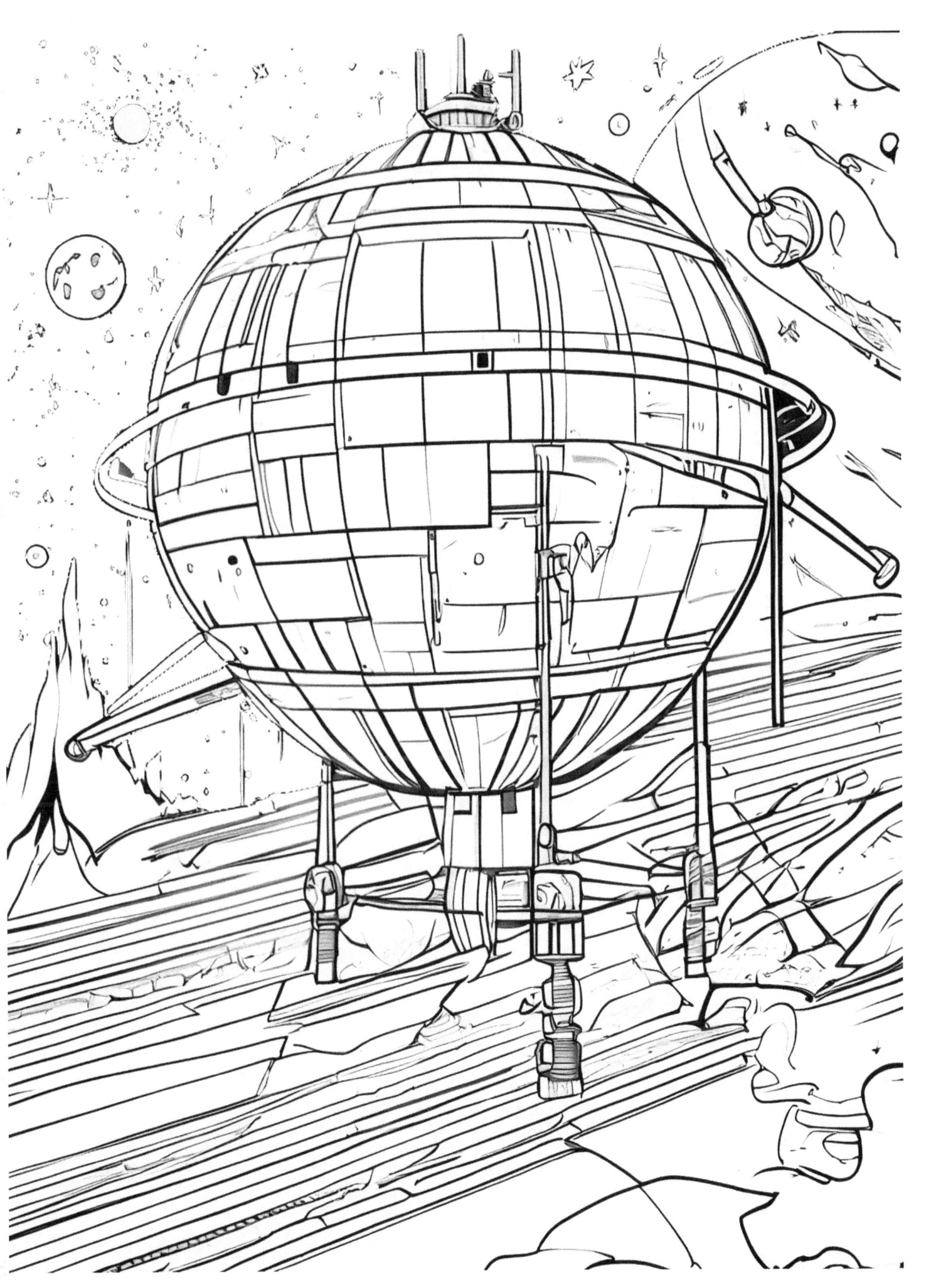

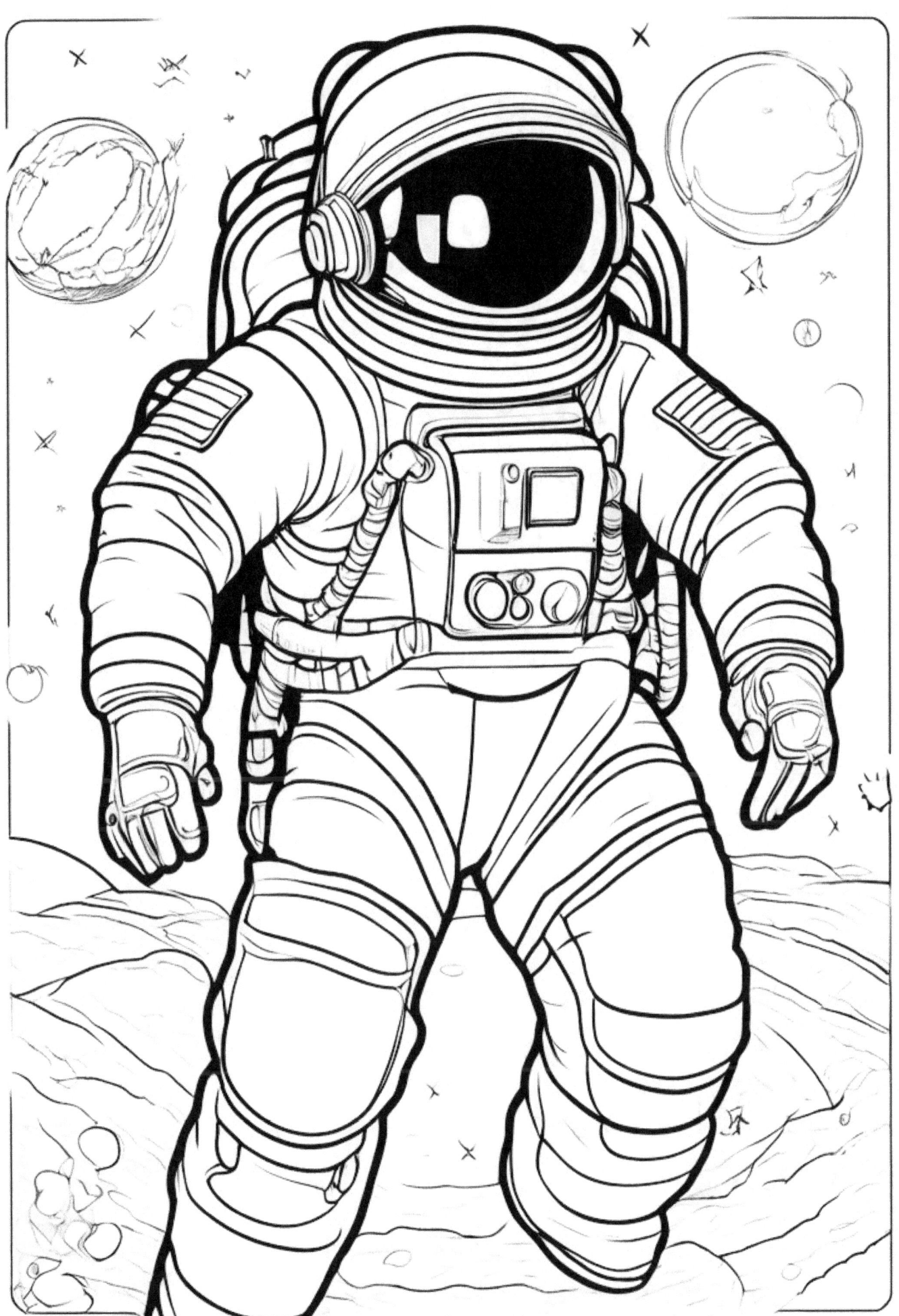

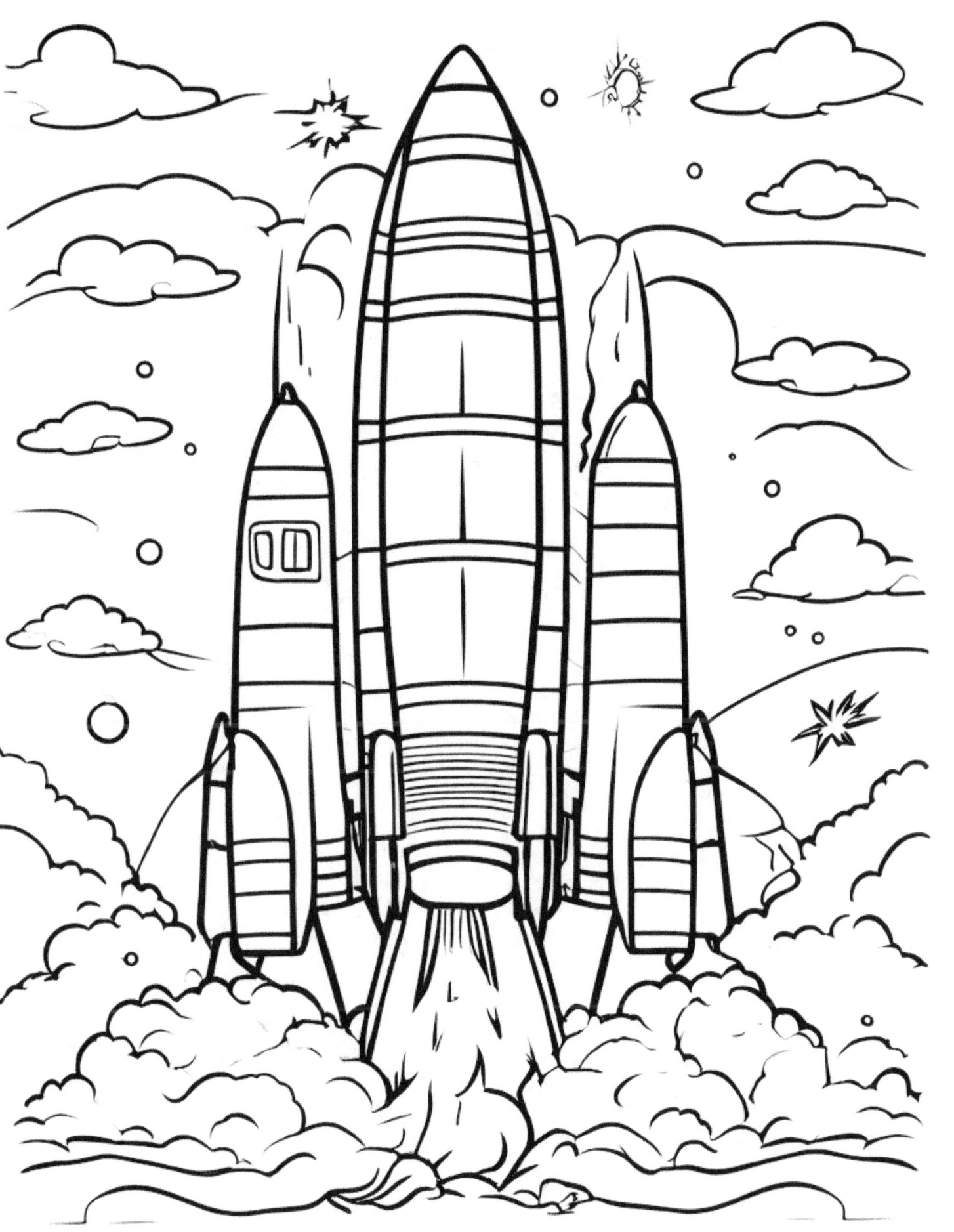

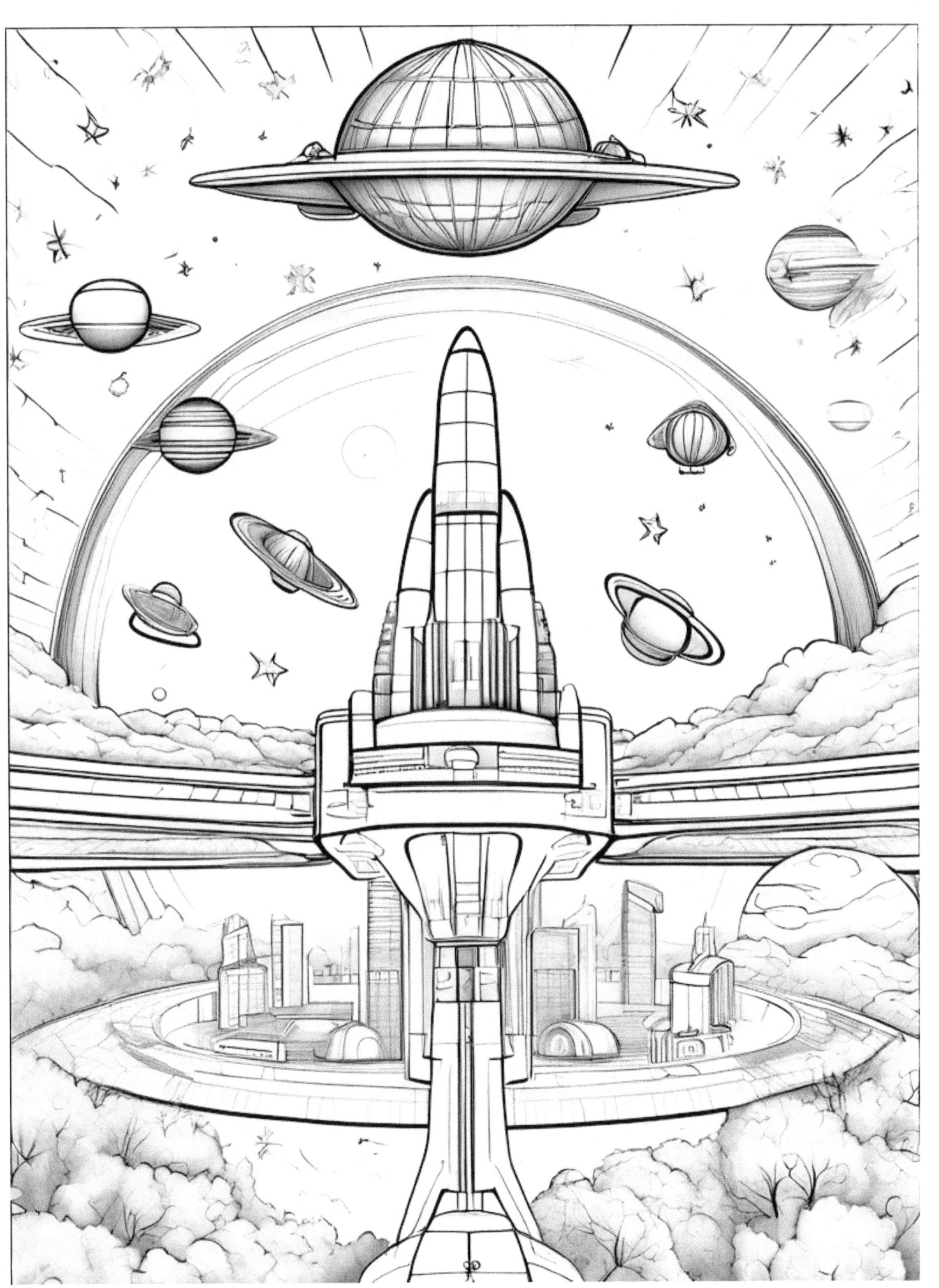

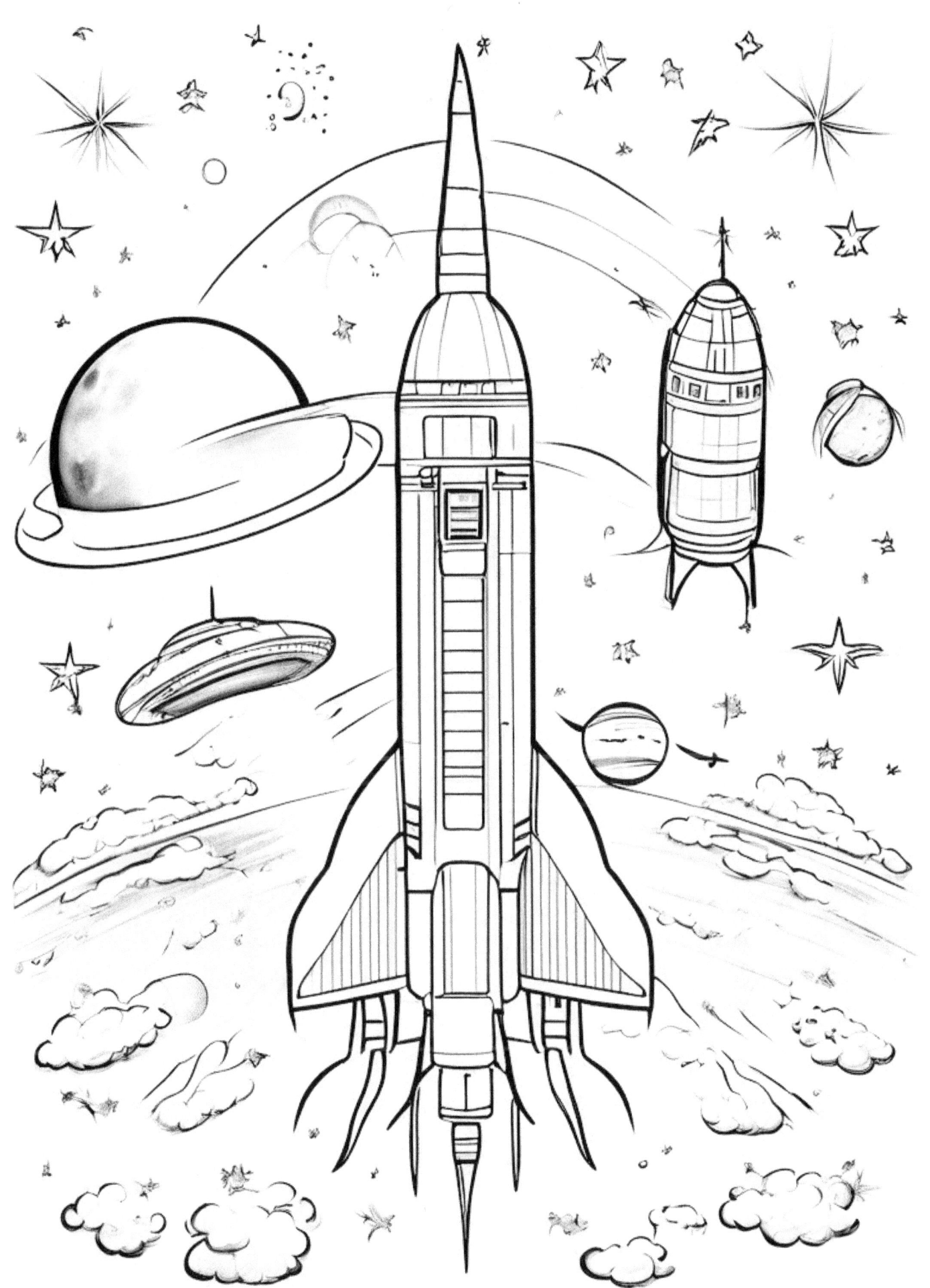

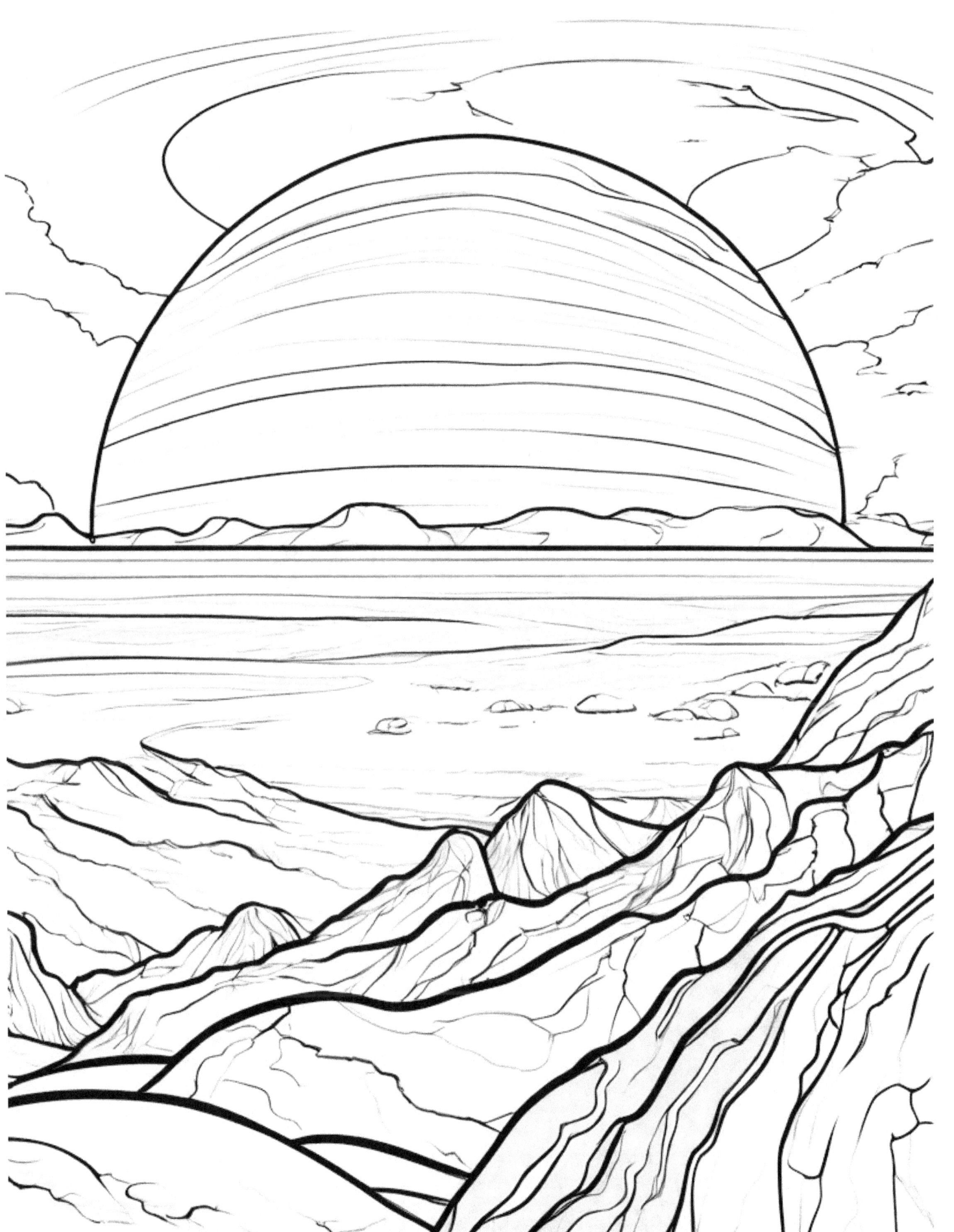

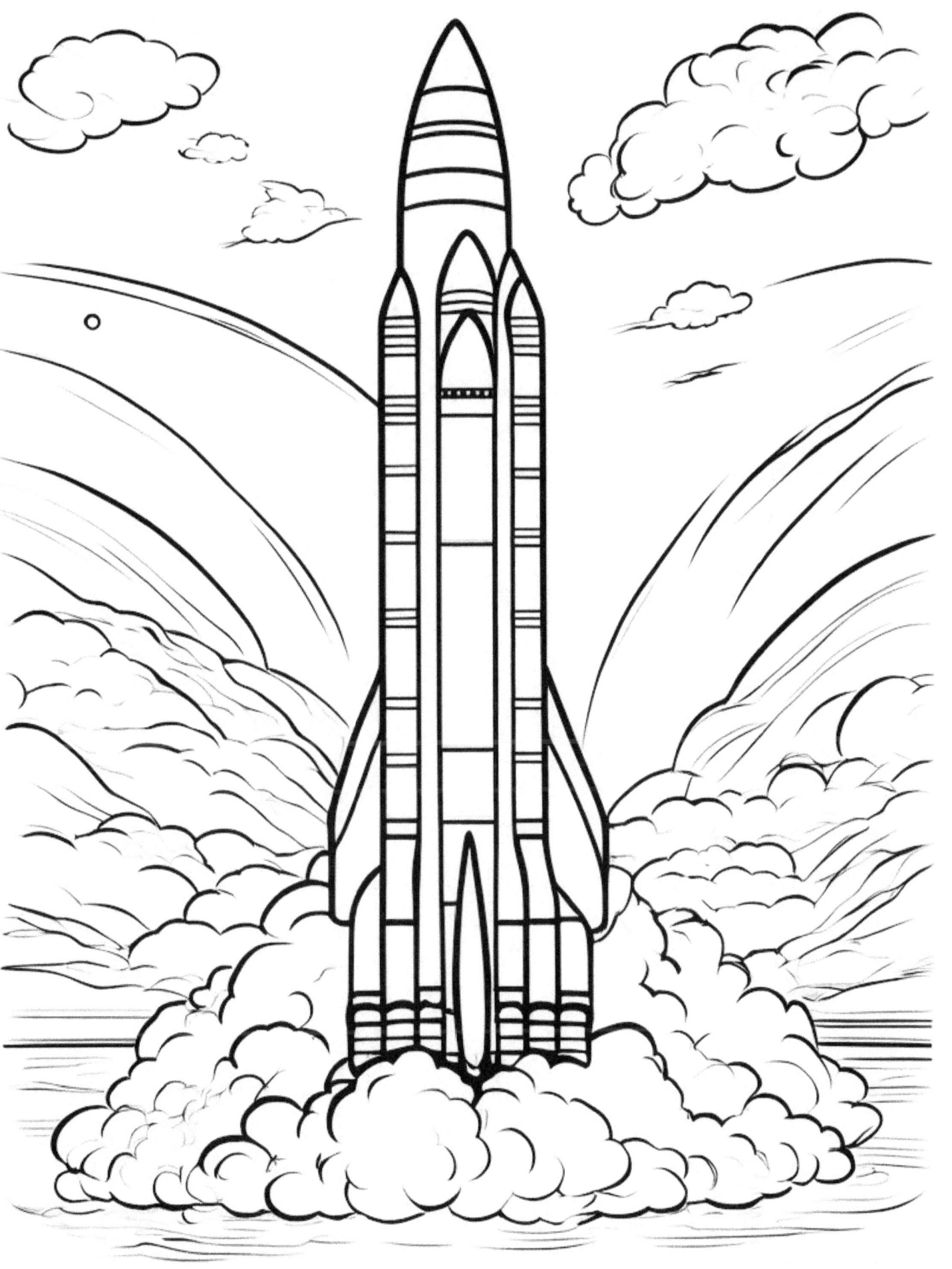

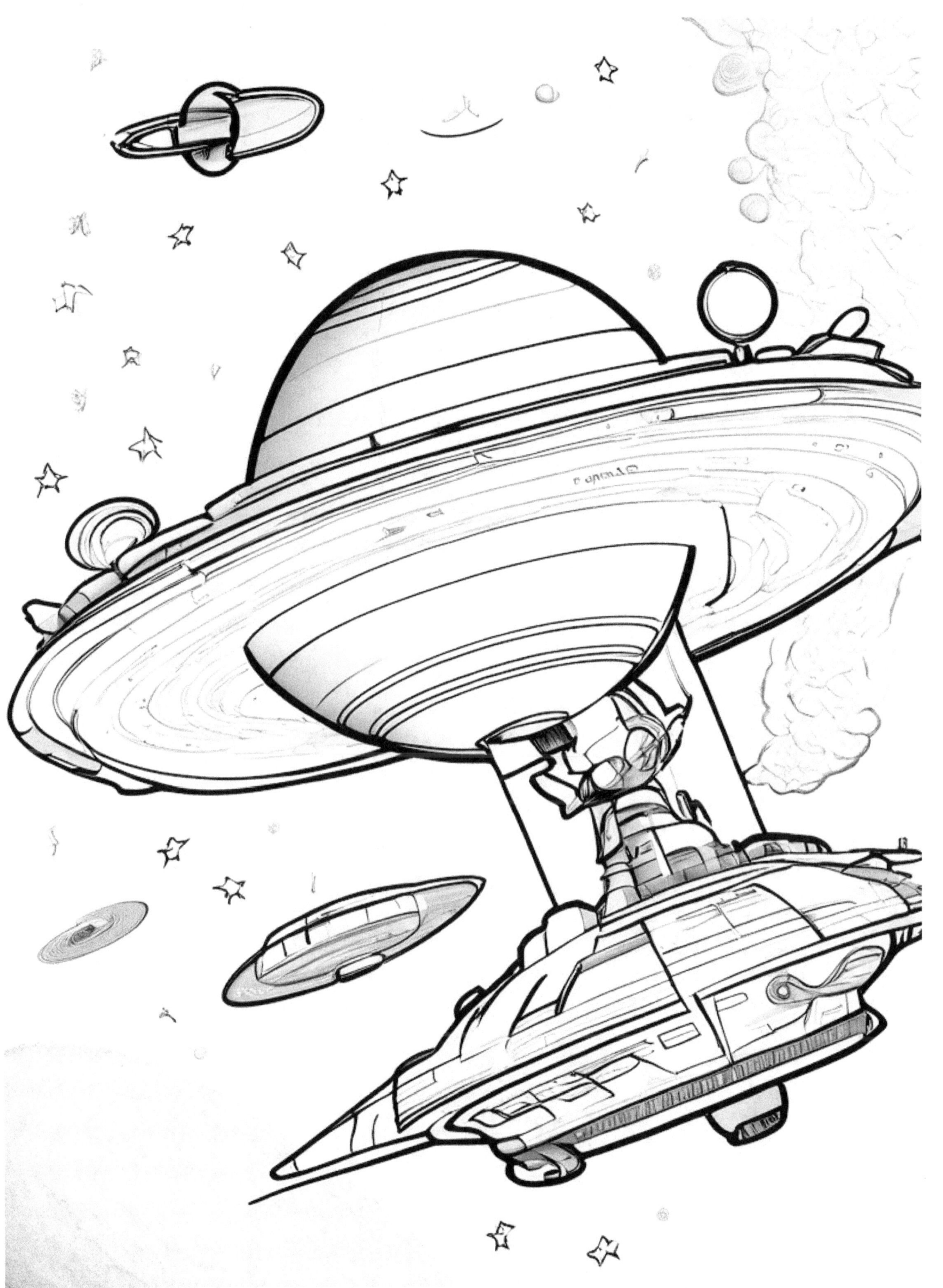

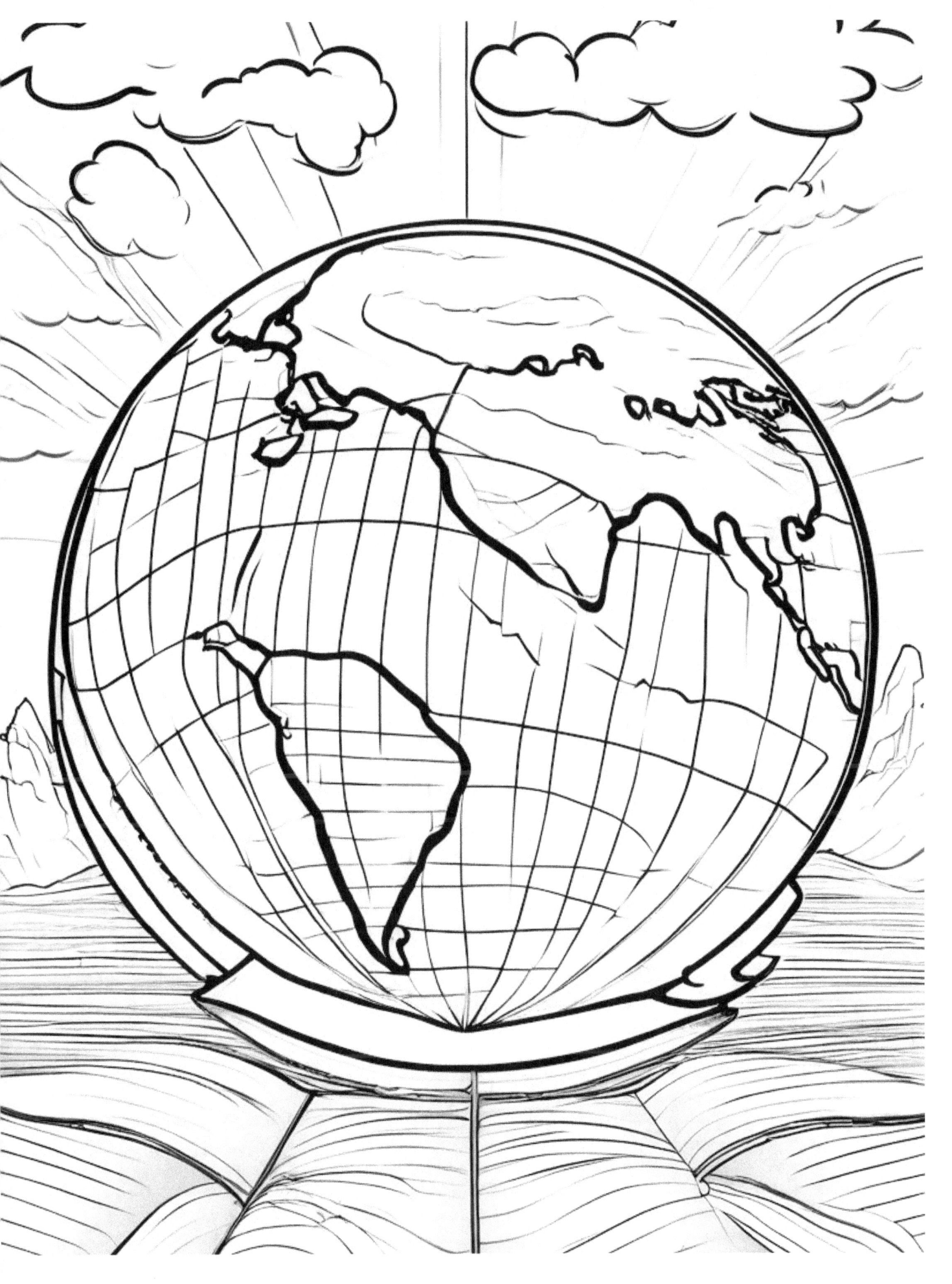

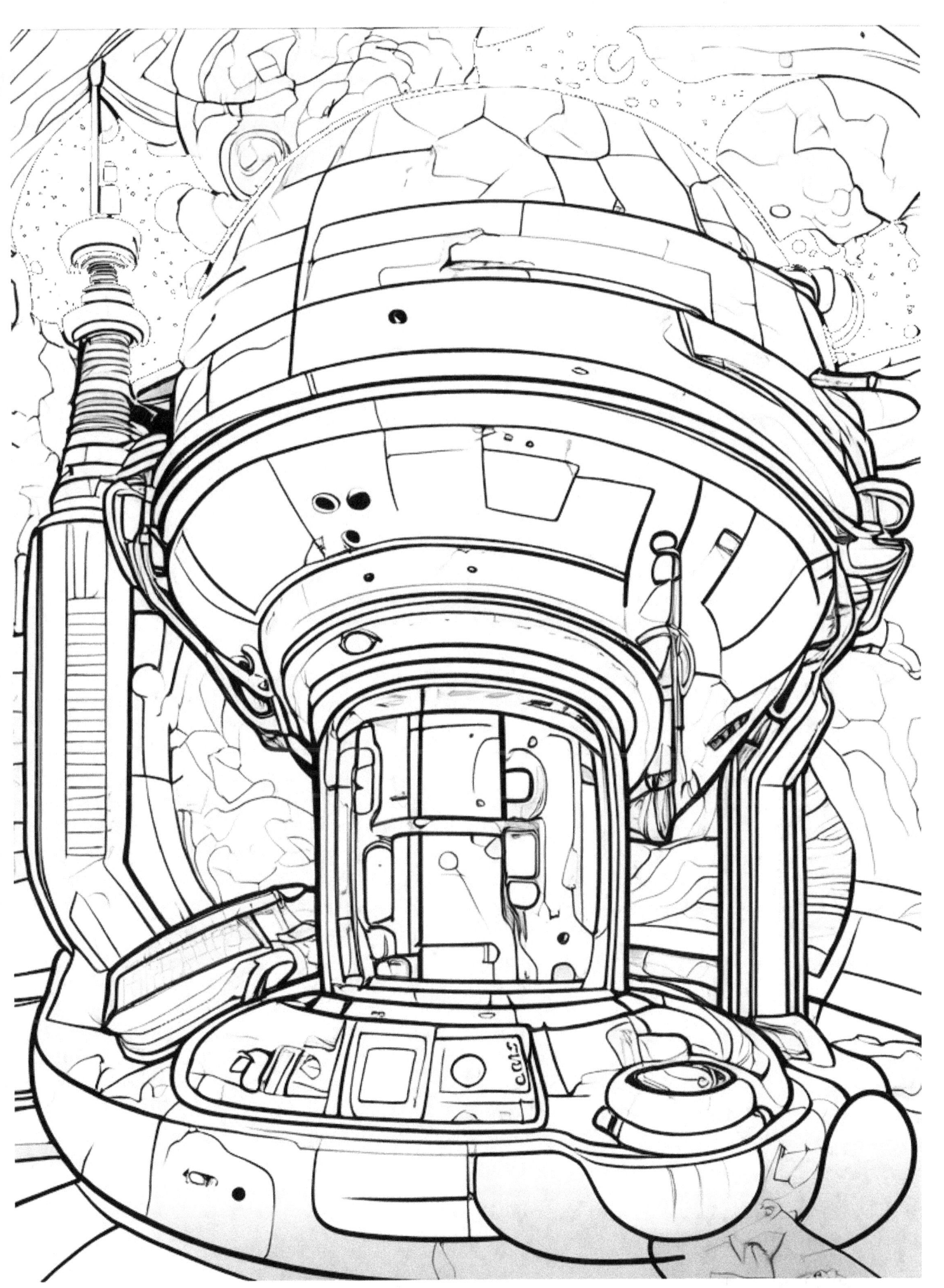

www.ingramcontent.com/pod-product-compliance
Lightning Source LLC
Chambersburg PA
CBHW062112220526
45471CB00010B/3701